WOMEN IN THE NEW
TESTAMENT WORLD

ESSENTIALS OF BIBLICAL STUDIES

Series Editor

Patricia K. Tull, Louisville Presbyterian Theological Seminary

Women in the New Testament World

SUSAN E. HYLEN

OXFORD
UNIVERSITY PRESS

OXFORD
UNIVERSITY PRESS

Oxford University Press is a department of the University of Oxford. It furthers
the University's objective of excellence in research, scholarship, and education
by publishing worldwide. Oxford is a registered trade mark of Oxford University
Press in the UK and certain other countries.

Published in the United States of America by Oxford University Press
198 Madison Avenue, New York, NY 10016, United States of America.

© Oxford University Press 2019

Library of Congress Cataloging-in-Publication Data
Names: Hylen, Susan, author.
Title: Women in the New Testament World / Susan E. Hylen.
Description: New York : Oxford University Press, 2018. |
Series: Essentials of biblical studies |
Includes bibliographical references and index.
Identifiers: LCCN 2018009551 | ISBN 9780190237578 (hardcover : alk. paper) |
ISBN 9780190237585 (pbk. : alk. paper) | ISBN 9780190237615 (online resource)
Subjects: LCSH: Women in the Bible. | Bible.
New Testament—Criticism, interpretation, etc.
Classification: LCC BS575 .H95 2018 | DDC 225.9/5082—dc23
LC record available at https://lccn.loc.gov/2018009551

1 3 5 7 9 8 6 4 2

Paperback printed by Sheridan Books, Inc., United States of America
Hardback printed by Bridgeport National Bindery, Inc., United States of America

For Marian and Maria

CONTENTS

FIGURES

ACKNOWLEDGMENTS

The creation of a book is never a solo endeavor. I am grateful for the institutional and personal support I have received on many fronts. Emory University and Candler School of Theology provided me with regular leave time, research funding, and administrative support. In particular, the leadership of Dean Jan Love creates an environment where individual research can thrive. In countless ways, Candler's administrators and staff attend to the needs of the school and in doing so make possible my research and writing. My faculty colleagues are generous with their time and always willing to offer concrete assistance as well as moral support. I am privileged to work in such a supportive environment, and I am grateful that I do.

My research for this particular project benefited greatly from the resources of the Pitts Theology Library. The library staff were very knowledgeable and always willing to help. In addition, the resources and staff of Emory's Carlos Museum were valuable. My research assistants, Aaron Carr and Nick Cupp, helped me track down inscriptions and read drafts of the manuscript. Professor Shively Smith of Wesley Theological Seminary offered collegial support and thoughtful feedback on my work.

I am especially thankful for the support of my family. My partner, Ted Smith, makes my work possible in countless ways through his care for me and our household. Our sons, Bennett and Tobias, are amazing individuals whose love and affection I depend on. This book is dedicated to two talented women: my mother, Marian Hylen, and my sister, Maria Simili. They are models of faith and leadership for me and for many others. Their encouragement and love are a source of strength for which I am grateful.

ABBREVIATIONS

Abbreviations of journals and ancient texts follow the conventions of the *SBL Handbook of Style* (2nd ed., Atlanta: SBL Press, 2014). Works not listed there are abbreviated according to the conventions of *A Patristic Greek Lexicon*, edited by G. W. H. Lampe (Oxford: Clarendon Press, 1968). Papyri are abbreviated according to the *Checklist of Editions of Greek and Latin Papyri, Ostraca, and Tablets,* online at http://library.duke.edu/rubenstein/scriptorium/papyrus/texts/clist.html. Ancient works not listed in these sources are found below.

ATh   *Acts of Paul and Thecla.*

Bloch   *The Roman Brick Stamps,* ed. Herbert Bloch
             (Rome: L'Erma de Bretschneider, 1967).

Cod. Just. *Corpus Iuris Civilis,* vol. 2, *Codex Iustinainus,* ed.
             Paul Krueger (Berolini: Apud Weidmannos, 1906).

Dig.   *The Digest of Justinian,* Latin text, ed. Theodor
             Mommsen (Berlin: Weidmann, 1868);
             repr. with English trans., ed. Alan Watson
             (Philadelphia: University of Pennsylvania
             Press, 1985).

DJD   *Discoveries in the Judean Desert* (Oxford: Oxford
          University Press, 1955–2011).

Eph.   *An Ephesian Tale* by Xenophon of Ephesus.

Frag.   C. Musonius Rufus, *Reliquiae*, ed. O. Hense
          (Lipsiae: in aedibus B. G. Teubneri, 1905; repr.
          Leipzig: Teubner, 1990).

ILS   *Inscriptiones Latinae Selectae*, ed. Hermann Dessau,
          3 vols. (Berolini: Apud Weidmannos, 1892–1916).

Pleket *Epigraphica II: Texts on the Social History of the Greek
          World*, ed. H. W. Pleket (Leiden: Brill, 1969).

Pont.   Ovid, *Epistulae ex Ponto* (*Letters from the Black Sea*).

RIC   *The Roman Imperial Coinage*. Harold Mattingly
          and Edward A. Sydenham, vol. 2 (London: Spink &
          Son, 1926).

TAM   *Tituli Asiae Minoris* (Vienna: Verlag der
          Österreichischen Akademie der Wissenschaften, 1901–).

SERIES INTRODUCTION

The past three decades have seen an explosion of approaches to study of the Bible, as older exegetical methods have been joined by a variety of literary, anthropological, and social models. Interfaith collaboration has helped change the field, and the advent of more cultural diversity among biblical scholars in the West and around the world has broadened our reading and interpretation of the Bible. These changes have also fueled interest in Scripture's past: both the ancient Near Eastern and Mediterranean worlds out of which Scripture came and the millennia of premodern interpretation through which it traveled to our day. The explosion of information and perspectives is so vast that no one textbook can any longer address the many needs of seminaries and colleges where the Bible is studied.

In addition to these developments in the field itself are changes in the students. Traditionally the domain of seminaries, graduate schools, and college and university religion classes, now biblical study also takes place in a host of alternative venues. As lay leadership in local churches develops, nontraditional, weekend, and online preparatory classes have mushroomed. As seminaries in Africa, Asia, and Latin America grow, particular need for inexpensive, easily available materials is clear. As religious controversies over the Bible's origins and norms continue to dominate the air-waves, congregation members and even curious nonreligious folk seek reliable paths into particular topics. And teachers themselves continue to seek guidance in areas of the ever-expanding field of scriptural study with which they may be less than familiar.

A third wave of changes also makes this series timely: shifts in the publishing industry itself. Technologies and knowledge are shifting so rapidly that large books are out of date almost before they are in print. The internet and the growing popularity of e-books call for flexibility and accessibility in marketing and sales. If the days when one expert can sum up the field in a textbook are gone, also gone are the days when large, expensive multi-authored tomes are attractive to students, teachers, and other readers.

During my own years of seminary teaching, I have tried to find just the right book or books for just the right price, at just the right reading level for my students, with just enough information to orient them without drowning them in excess reading. For all the reasons stated above, this search was all too often less than successful. So I was excited to be asked to help Oxford University Press assemble a select crew of leading scholars to create a series that would respond to such classroom challenges. Essentials of Biblical Studies comprises freestanding, relatively brief, accessibly written books that provide orientation to the Bible's contents, its ancient contexts, its interpretive methods and history, and its themes and figures. Rather than a one-size-had-better-fit-all approach, these books may be mixed and matched to suit the objectives of a variety of classroom venues as well as the needs of individuals wishing to find their way into unfamiliar topics.

I am confident that our book authors will join me in returning enthusiastic thanks to the editorial staff at Oxford University Press for their support and guidance, especially Theo Calderara, who shepherded the project in its early days, and Dr. Steve Wiggins, who has been a most wise and steady partner in this work since joining OUP in 2013.

Patricia K. Tull
Editor

Chapter 1

Introduction

MANY READERS OF THE NEW Testament seek a deeper understanding of the women—or the statements about women—that appear in these texts. As they do so, they often seek information about the social context in which the New Testament was written. The authors of the New Testament writings shared the same social background as their readers. They took for granted that those early readers would use cultural knowledge to understand their message. Readers today, who have different assumptions and experiences of gender roles and expectations, often desire additional knowledge of the historical context in order to interpret these writings.

Consider this example: the Gospel of Luke indicated that there were women who traveled with Jesus and his disciples and who "provided for them out of their resources" (Luke 8:3). The author did not comment on this practice as if it were unusual and assumed the reader's cultural knowledge of such customs. Modern readers may desire to know more about the social conventions that shaped the women's provision. What kinds of resources were women likely to have? What relationships were implied by such an arrangement? The reader who understands the historical context can better judge what kind of connection these women may have had to the Jesus movement.

Another example is Lydia, who was described as a businesswoman and the head of her household. She prevailed upon Paul and his companions to stay with her in Philippi (Acts

16:14–15). Without some knowledge of the cultural context, it is difficult to know whether it was common for women to be heads of households, to run businesses, or to offer hospitality to traveling teachers. Readers may wonder whether Lydia was married, who the members of her household were, or what kind of relationship was implied between Lydia and Paul.

Cultural background, then, helps the reader to "fill in the gaps" left by the writer, who presumes common knowledge that modern readers do not share. Researching the social practices of the time cannot offer single, definitive answers to many of the questions modern readers have. Instead, this exploration helps us understand the ideas and practices early readers were likely to be familiar with. For example, the social status of the women who provided for Jesus is difficult to define with much certainty. Among the women Luke 8:3 lists was Joanna, the wife of Chuza, Herod's steward. This woman was someone who might have had political influence. Yet not enough information is given to determine many aspects of her social status, such as the level of her wealth. Similarly, there is no historical evidence that can help us determine Lydia's marital status with any certainty. Even readers who understand first-century practices of marriage and widowhood will not know definitively if Lydia was married. But they may be better able to determine what the options were in her context, or what Luke's readers were likely to understand about her.

A broader sense of the culture that produced the New Testament may also help modern readers avoid mistaken assumptions about women in this period. It is not uncommon to find New Testament interpreters making assertions that do not fit the first-century context. For example, some writers have assumed that women were legally subject to their husbands' authority, that husbands controlled their wives' property, or that women were not allowed to initiate a divorce. None of these things were strictly true of the first-century Roman world, as women had a greater degree of legal independence and social influence at that time than in many cultures before or since.

For example, interpreters of 1 Timothy have often compared the language of the letter to its cultural background. How did the author's assertion that women should not speak or have authority over men (1 Tim 2:11–12) fit within other cultural norms and practices? Raymond Collins situated the language of 1 Tim 2:11–12 within this background: "In the Greco-Roman household, the *paterfamilias* exercised virtually absolute authority not only over his children but also over his wife."[1] Collins asserted that the letter's instructions would appear conventional to its early readers. Although Collins's interpretation has many merits, his description of marriage is problematic. The form of marriage he described, in which the legal authority of the father transferred to the husband at marriage, was no longer commonly practiced in the first century. As I describe in chapter 4, contemporary marriage practices granted women considerably more legal autonomy than Collins suggested. The legal independence of women from their husbands had a significant effect on the activities women undertook, even though their subordination to their husbands was still assumed to be the ideal. A different understanding of the social background may help readers understand the instructions about women's silence in a new way.

In another example from 1 Timothy, Risto Saarinen argued that the women deacons mentioned in 1 Tim 3:11 must have been unmarried women, because "a married woman was obliged to devote herself to her own household."[2] However, there is substantial evidence that women served in religious and civic offices in this region and time period, and that their capacity to hold office was not determined by their marital status.[3] Indeed, a good deal of evidence comes from Ephesus, the location of the community 1 Timothy addressed. If the author disagreed with local expectations that married and unmarried women exercised a variety of civic and religious offices, he might have specified how Christian practices should differ. Yet the writer said only that deacons should be married once, leaving open the possibility that they were either married or widowed. Drawing a richer portrait of the gendered practices of the time period can affect the interpreter's understanding of the roles of women deacons in 1 Timothy.

The task of this book is to provide as clear a picture as possible of the legal and social status of women. This cultural backdrop prepares readers of the New Testament to make interpretive decisions about the language of the New Testament. Such information does not give definitive answers to many questions readers have, but it can provide new insights into a passage, and it can help them avoid mistakes.

Before diving into a discussion of social status or marriage customs, however, this chapter introduces readers to questions that arise in approaching the subject of women in the ancient world and to the sources of evidence that are available for study. The first two sections below take up the terms of the book's title: "Women" and "the New Testament World." Both terms present distinct challenges for the historian. Although "women" can seem easy to identify in history, it is difficult to explore this ancient category without importing contemporary biases. The first section provides questions and tools needed to approach the study of women. The second section introduces readers to the complexity and scope of the New Testament world. It outlines the time frame, geography, and some important cultural influences in the context of the New Testament. There was a great deal of cultural change going on in this time period. These changes affected the lives of women, and they should also shape the way modern readers approach the evidence for women's lives.

Last, the third section introduces readers to the evidence available for women's lives in the period. There is very little direct evidence for women's lives. Some women certainly wrote about their lives in diaries, but unfortunately none have survived. While numerous sources of evidence are available, each comes with its own particular problems of interpretation. The final section presents the types of evidence available for study and the difficulties associated with each.

WOMEN AS A HISTORICAL SUBJECT

Readers who are new to the scholarly study of ancient women may not stop to wonder how to study women in history. The answer to the question "What is a woman?" may seem self-evident. If pressed to define the term "woman," some would give an answer determined by biology: a woman is a person with two X chromosomes. Modern writers often employ categories like "men" and "women" and assume that readers understand what these terms mean without defining them.

Some modern readers examine the evidence for women in antiquity without asking the question "What is a woman?" And, indeed, it is possible to proceed in this way. There were people in antiquity whom we would identify as male and female in the same ways we identify people today. What is more, ancient people had words for women and men, male and female, and so forth. They gave children names that were gender specific. If modern interpreters want to explore these categories, it should be easy enough to identify these groups in the historical record.

Yet the question "What is a woman?" is still worth pausing over for a moment. This volume explores how people in the cultures that produced the New Testament understood what it meant to be a woman—not what we assume to be true about women today. We ask the question "What is a woman?" not because we do not have an answer, nor because we think the ancients did not, but because we want to piece together from another culture's perspective what it meant to be male and female.[4] It is precisely because we often take our own understanding of sex and gender for granted that we should stop and consider the possibility that this knowledge is particular to our own time and place.

In fact, scholars often point to ancient Greece and Rome as examples of cultural understandings of sex and gender that are very different from modern notions. In 1990, Thomas Laqueur argued that the ancient Greeks and Romans conceived of sex and gender very differently from people today. Instead of two distinct biological sexes, there was only one. The male sex was normative, and females were simply a subset of the male. Laqueur showed that authors like the fourth-century B.C.E. philosopher Aristotle and the second-century C.E. physician Galen understood male and female reproductive anatomy to be identical—except that the female's was interior instead of exterior to the body. "Instead of being divided by their reproductive anatomies, the sexes are linked by a common one."[5] Laqueur concluded that in these centuries "woman does not exist as an ontologically distinct category."[6] This conception was very different from modern formulations of sex and gender.

The ancient conception of sex that Laqueur traced was also different from modern notions because it was inherently hierarchical. It assumed that women were biologically inferior to men. In a classic example, Aristotle wrote, "The female is as it were a deformed male" (*Gen. an.* 2.3 [737a28]). As Laqueur argued, the ancients saw women as "inverted and hence less perfect men."[7] This hierarchical understanding was widely shared in ancient sources.

In a similar vein, David Halperin argued that ancient Greeks and Romans had a distinctive view of gender. (By "gender," I mean the social roles and values associated with being male and female. It would also be possible to explore non-binary gender expressions in antiquity, but that subject lies outside the scope of the current volume.) Writing in the same year as Laqueur, Halperin focused his attention on ancient sexuality. He argued that the ancients had no category comparable to our "sexuality." They did not categorize people according to a preference for male or female sexual partners, nor did they view such a preference as an "orientation" that was part of one's "identity."[8] In making this argument, Halperin also displayed important elements of ancient views of gender. What was important to the ancients in sexual partners was not whether the partner was male or female but who took the "active" role, which they understood as the one who sexually penetrated the other. For ancient writers, being active was, by definition, a male role. Therefore, men who were penetrated by other men took on the "passive" role and thus were feminine. But the ancients saw nothing unusual in men who penetrated other men because they played the active, masculine role. Halperin showed that categories like active and passive helped define what it meant to be male or female.

The one-sex model is a helpful reminder not to import modern assumptions, even of such basic questions as what constitutes male and female. The historian's task is to try to see the ancient world from within—to try to understand the way people conceived of gender or how they attached value to it— rather than to impose our own conceptions and values. Recent scholarship has argued in multiple instances that sex and gender are socially constructed. That is, what it means to be male or female is not a biologically given category that endures through time but is constructed by culture, often with political, social, and religious ramifications. In every culture, people make sense of their experiences and the world around them, and in doing so they construct understandings of what it means to be male or female.

The one-sex model is also important because it illustrates how the definition of male and female is not simply given but serves the interests of some members of society. Because the ancient views seem foreign to us, it is easy to see how their descriptions of male and female differences served their own social and political needs. (It is much more difficult to see this about our own views of gender.) The ancient writers assumed the superiority of men over women, and they inscribed this hierarchy onto their observations of the human body.[9] Males could conceivably have been described as inverted females, with the female anatomy assumed to be nor- mative and the male's its inverse. But this would likely never have occurred to the ancients, who were already convinced of female inferiority. Even on matters about which the ancient authors differ—for example, whether women were cold by nature and men hot, or vice versa—they agreed that whichever qualities were viewed as inherently male were of greater value.[10] Descriptions of sex and gender were not neutral but reinforced social and political structures.

Although the one-sex model can help modern readers encounter some of our own biases, it is limited in helping us understand the lives of ancient women. This model may not have been the only way ancient people understood sex and gender. Classicist Helen King has shown evidence of more than one view of gender in the ancient world. She argued that Hippocrates' medical writings "assumed that women are not just cold men, but are creatures entirely different from men in the texture of their flesh and in the associated physiological functions."[11] Although Laqueur argued that the idea that men and women were two sexes was a relatively recent phenomenon, King showed that multiple views existed in antiquity as well.

In addition, the focus on philosophical and medical writers can wrongly give the impression that women's lives were unchanging over many centuries. Some authors have pointed to the persistence of the one-sex model over time: from Aristotle, who lived and wrote in the fourth century B.C.E., to the second-century medical writer Galen. Galen's perspective intentionally repeated Aristotle's and drew further conclusions on the basis of these ideas. But tracing the dots between these two philosophers five centuries apart provides little information about the lives of actual women. Ancient sources like these showed a remarkable agreement about gender norms and virtues across many centuries. But if we look only at these sources, we will miss the considerable changes in the legal and social status of women. By the time Galen was writing, women had a very different legal and social position from that of their predecessors in Athens or Rome. Even if this view of physiology had not changed much, many elements of women's lives had changed.

To get a bigger picture of women's lives in this period, we need to put evidence of the legal, social, and material conditions of women's lives alongside philosophical conceptions of sex and gender. The idea that gender is socially constructed is important. However, the factors that led to the construction and performance of gender were shaped not only by the decree of philosophers but also by a host of social norms, legal structures, and political forces. Chapters 3 through 7 explore aspects of women's lives in the period. The sources of evidence for these topics are discussed later in this chapter.

This multifaceted approach shares a good deal in common with recent work in feminist studies and masculinity studies. Masculinity studies emerged in the 1990s out of the recognition that gender studies often focused solely on the female, while maleness remained invisible as a gender. This approach analyzes the construction and performance of masculinity, often similar to the way that feminists approach the study of being female.[12] These studies often acknowledge the importance of institutions, roles, behaviors, and values in addition to philosophical constructions of gender.[13]

Taking legal and social situations into account complicates the project of this book because women had different social and legal standings, depending on various factors. Some of the more important variables in this period were wealth, location, family of origin, slave versus free status, and citizenship. Gender ideology was important, but it was not the only factor that shaped people's lives. Experiences of being female differed greatly. An exploration of women in the New Testament period will need to make room for this variety.

THE NEW TESTAMENT WORLD AS A HISTORICAL SUBJECT

The phrase "the New Testament World" serves as a kind of shorthand to identify the content of this book. It refers to the cultural context in which the books of the New Testament were written. Trying to understand the ways women were represented in the New Testament requires attention to the political, social, and legal positions of women in the culture at large. Even if early Christians innovated distinctive roles for women, they would have communicated these changes through language that made sense to people of that time period. The New Testament would reflect already existing social roles, patterns, and values to convey its message.

The New Testament writings were produced in the first century C.E., the period of Roman domination across the Mediterranean. Some scholars have argued that individual books were composed in the second century. This book considers evidence from the first century B.C.E. to the second century C.E., which historians call the early Roman period. This range allows for a variety of evidence to provide a context in which we can situate the New Testament writings. Even within this relatively narrow window, however, differences in date and of geographic location should shape the interpretation of the evidence.

The period of the New Testament corresponds to the establishment of the Roman Empire. In 27 B.C.E., the emperor Augustus became the sole leader in Rome, marking a change from the Republican period of Rome's history to the Imperial period. The change occurred alongside the consolidation of Rome's power across a wide territory, including the lands associated with the New Testament: Greece, Asia Minor, Egypt, and Judea.

The establishment of Augustus's rule came with many social changes and innovations, both in Rome and across the empire. The first century saw many structural changes in cities, as Roman and local elites built roads, aqueducts, theaters, baths, temples, and other monumental structures. There were also social changes, as people adapted to the concentration of power in the emperor and sought to curry favor with him or his representatives. Roman citizenship became an important marker of status and spread gradually throughout the empire as it was conferred by the emperor on his non-Roman allies. It was a time of relative prosperity compared to other pre-industrial societies.

Despite these changes, many elements of local cultures also remained in place. Roman law applied to all Roman citizens, but many of the inhabitants of the cities and territories Rome ruled were governed by local customs. Many of the legal norms of interest in this book, such as marriage and divorce, or the guardianship of women, fell into this category. Thus a number of different norms and practices existed simultaneously within the empire.

However, people in the provinces also took on aspects of Roman culture as a way of integrating into Roman rule. Although Roman expansion began with military conquest, the influence of Roman culture was not accomplished by force but through other means. Local leaders in the provinces drew from both Roman social mores and their own local practices to forge alliances with Rome and to reap the benefits Rome offered.[14] In many of the Roman provinces, inscriptions suggested that patterns of women's property ownership and patronage mirrored those of Roman law, even when the women involved were not always Roman citizens (see chapters 4 and 5).

Greek culture and language remained influential in this period. Many of these territories were already Greek-speaking or bilingual. Instead of imposing its own language, Latin, Rome continued the use of Greek in addition to Latin. Greek literature and philosophy were highly regarded. Thus, while many of the legal codes of the period were written in Latin, philosophical and literary texts, letters, and local court documents were often written in Greek, and sometimes in other local languages.

The writings of the New Testament reflected and spoke to this time period. The New Testament texts told stories of Jesus's life in Judea and the Galilee. Others were letters and sermons written to churches in Greece and Asia Minor. Cities like Alexandria in Egypt and Antioch in Syria have been suggested as locations of the writing of some of the New Testament books. These writings reflected knowledge of Rome as the center of political power at that time. They were written in Greek, the language that remained dominant during Roman rule.

The wide scope of the New Testament world presents a difficulty for exploring the lives of women. The evidence available came from a wide geographic area. Roman imperial rule brought many changes to the Mediterranean, but it did not require uniformity in many of the cultural practices that are central to this book. People in different places and times may have had different practices and values that shaped them as women and men.

Because practices varied from region to region, historians must look within a region for evidence of similarities and differences. For example, local Jewish practices seem to have allowed polygamy, even though Roman law did not permit it for Roman citizens. This is an example in which some of the local culture's marriage practices continued to exist.

However, this does not mean that local traditions were altogether different. Modern readers need to be especially careful about our assumptions regarding Jewish practices. We tend to expect that the Old Testament legal texts described the lives of all Jewish women in the first century. Old Testament laws were interpreted in a variety of ways to begin with, but Jewish communities were also affected by the cultures around them. For example, Jewish women owned and inherited property, as did their Roman and Greek counterparts. And elite Jewish women divorced and remarried in the same ways that Roman women did. Jewish communities may have retained some distinctive practices, but there was also a great deal of variety, including many practices that were widely shared across the subcultures of the Mediterranean. In exploring the lives of women, this book looks for both similarities and differences across regions.

EVIDENCE FOR THE LIVES OF WOMEN IN THE EARLY ROMAN PERIOD

Exploring questions of women in ancient history has always been difficult. The available sources are limited, and they offer only partial glimpses of women's lives. Women appeared less frequently than men in the historical record. Many of the sources were written by upper-class men and offer, at best, a biased picture of elite women's lives. Nevertheless, over the past forty years historians have made important strides in uncovering and interpreting evidence of women's lives. In doing so, they enabled a new set of questions to emerge, so that interpreting the evidence for women's lives in the first century remains a challenging and interesting task.

A primary problem for the historian interested in women's lives in antiquity is simply the quantity of evidence that is available. The limited amount of evidence is due to a number of factors. Most of the architecture and artifacts of antiquity have not survived to the present. The sparse evidence available presents a limited picture and may skew the results in particular ways.

This section describes the kinds of evidence available for understanding what women's lives were like in this period. It also explores some of the inherent problems the evidence poses for answering the questions that modern readers have. First, there are philosophical, historical, and literary works, which for various reasons were deemed important enough to be retained and transmitted through the years. Second, there are inscriptions marking burial sites, commemorative statues, or buildings. These items were not always preserved intentionally, and indeed were often moved from their original location. Third, papyrus documents have been discovered in the north African and Judean deserts. In the dry climate there, organic material decays very slowly. Some papyrus fragments were intentionally preserved in archives and others were thrown away as garbage but unearthed by archaeologists.

The publication of inscriptions yields new kinds of information for assessing women's lives. Inscriptions were made for a variety of purposes. Some of the most common were inscriptions marking gravesites and honoring the deceased, and inscriptions that named important donors and honored their civic contributions. Such inscriptions were costly and thus represented a segment of the population with disposable income. Yet they nevertheless included a population of both local elite and sub-elite people.

Similarly, papyrus documents give a different understanding of the lives of people in this period. Some papyri were letters noting mundane topics like the care of farm animals and the sale of goods. Others were receipts for the payment of taxes and loans, or legal documents like wills and dowry arrangements. Many came from the nonelite layers of society, people whom the philosophical authors largely ignored. Some were written by the sender; others were written by a paid scribe because the sender was either illiterate or not literate enough to write a formal document. These records survived only in places like Egypt and the Judean desert, where the dryness of the climate preserves organic materials like paper. They are geographically limited but often allow important insights into the lives of people from various classes of society.

In the chapters that follow, I have cited a published translation of the ancient sources whenever possible. Readers who do not read Greek or Latin may want to access these sources for further information, or to get a sense of the work as a whole. Citations of these modern sources may be found in the endnotes.

Philosophical Writings and Letters

When scholars first turned significant attention to questions of women in history, they began with the most familiar and widely available sources. These were primarily literary texts written by well-educated, upper-class men. Men were more likely to be educated as statesmen and philosophers, and thus to write the philosophical texts and letters that later generations deemed important. These authors rarely wrote directly about women's lives. Instead, women were mentioned in passing, as tangential to the central subject matter. These writings generate specific kinds of insights and questions for modern readers. It can be difficult to know whether these sources conveyed reliable historical information about women or simply transmitted stereotypes and biases that were common at the time.

As an example, consider this quote from the Roman historian Livy. Livy wrote in the first century about a famous debate in the senate that took place in 195 B.C.E. He quoted Lucius Valerius, saying of women: "Never while their males survive is feminine slavery shaken off; and even they abhor the freedom which loss of husbands and fathers gives" (*Hist.* 34.7.12).[15] Valerius suggested that women preferred to live under the strict authority of their fathers or husbands.

Some early interpreters saw Livy as a reliable observer of culture. For example, writing in 1977, Marjorie Lightman and William Zeisel understood the quote this way: "Women, according to Lucius, willingly served men and abhorred the freedom that the death of a father or husband produced."[16] Like these historians, many interpreted authors like Livy as recording how households in antiquity functioned: the male heads of the household made all decisions, and wives carried them out. In this approach, Valerius's words reflected actual relationships between husbands and wives.

But historians have long recognized that such a straightforward reading of an author like Livy obscures some of the most important features of his work. Historians have come to consider the author's identity and social location along with the genre and rhetorical aims of the text. From an early point, feminist historians noted the problem of having source texts written almost exclusively by men. Even if Valerius understood women as happy participants in their subordination, his words do not tell us what the women themselves thought. The authors expressed ideas that were colored by their experiences as elite men.

Perhaps more important, the purpose of most literary sources was not to communicate information about men and women. These texts had rhetorical aims: they sought to persuade the reader of a certain viewpoint, to shed light on a social phenomenon, or to convey information the author deemed important or useful. In Livy's case, Lucius Valerius proposed the repeal of the Oppian laws, austerity measures passed in a time of war to marshal resources for the good of the city. The laws restricted the amount of gold a woman could wear, and forbade multicolored clothing and travel by carriage in or around Rome (Livy, *Hist.* 34.1.3). Repealing the laws would have allowed Romans greater freedom to display their wealth. Valerius's opponent, Cato, had warned that women would run rampant if given license to dress as they wished (see chapter 7). In response, Valerius asserted that women would remain under the authority of their husbands or fathers, an authority the women preferred to the restrictions of the Oppian laws. Valerius did not intend to describe actual relationships between women and men or women's feelings about the authority of their husbands. Instead, he sought to persuade other elite men that the repeal of the Oppian laws would not result in the problems Cato had identified.

These authors often mentioned women as a means of communicating other goals and not as the main subject of the work. For example, the early second-century Roman historian Suetonius wrote of the emperor Augustus: "The education of his daughter and granddaughters included even spinning and weaving; they were forbidden to say or do anything, either publicly or in private, that could not decently figure in the imperial day-book" (*Aug.* 64).[17] Suetonius wrote in praise of Augustus. He gave the emperor credit for a well-ordered household that exhibited traditional virtues. As such, his statement provides little real information about the activities of women in Augustus's family. Indeed, Suetonius also acknowledged accusations of vice against the same daughter and a granddaughter. But in this passage, he cast Augustus as the virtuous head of his household. The actions described illustrated classical virtues and thus honored both the women and the emperor.

Acknowledging the author's interests and aims allows for a different approach to ancient works as historical evidence. Instead of assuming that elite male authors accurately represented ancient cultures, the interpreter looks for social norms and values that the author and ancient readers shared. From Suetonius's statement about Augustus's household, modern readers learn that wool-working and silence were traditional virtues for women. Furthermore, these traits not only characterized women but were also used to praise men as good leaders of their households.

Ancient authors often presented idealized versions of historical events that reinforced the culture's gender norms. A further example comes from another story told by Suetonius. He recounts the tale of Claudia, "who, when the ship that was bringing the sacred emblems of the Idaean Mother Goddess to Rome grounded on a Tiber mudbank, publicly prayed that she might be allowed to refloat it in proof of her perfect chastity, and did so" (*Tib.* 2). Suetonius's miracle story will likely strike the modern reader as historically implausible. No existing historical evidence would confirm the veracity of the events Suetonius recalled.[18] If the historian is looking for facts in the events of Claudia's life, the sources offer little help.

However, historical information can still be gleaned from such a source. The interpreter asks what the author's rhetorical goals were in telling the story and what cultural knowledge he expected readers to use to achieve those aims. In this case, Suetonius praised Claudia (and through her, the Julio-Claudian line of emperors) for her chastity or sexual morality. Suetonius assumed the reader understood that chastity was a virtue and that they would not be surprised to find a god or goddess intervening in human affairs for the sake of chastity. Read in this way, the quote is useful as evidence of the social values that shaped the lives of women and men.

Fictional works are also a source of evidence for gender norms of the period. A number of Greek novels were written in the first and second centuries. These works were not meant to be taken as histories. The stories were implausible because of the high level of coincidental events. For example, Callirhoe married her husband Chaereas, who was consumed with jealousy and struck her. She was presumed dead and buried but was not actually dead. Before this could be discovered, grave robbers came and carried her away and sold her to Dionysius as a slave. Realizing she was pregnant by Chaereas, she allowed herself to be freed and married to the man who purchased her, though she always retained her love for Chaereas. And that was only the beginning of the tale! But although the stories were unlikely as a whole, individual events were meant to sound familiar. Bandits robbed graves and roamed the countryside, afflicting travelers. People were mistreated by others and petitioned the authorities for redress. Religious festivals occurred with pageantry and sacrificial offerings. The stories relied on the reader to recognize motivations of characters (like Chaereas's jealousy) or particular circumstances (being sold as a slave) as plausible. Because of this, we may analyze the narratives for the kinds of behavior that were assumed to be normal.

Understanding social history in this way requires the interpreter to develop a pattern of evidence seen across various sources. If Suetonius was the only one who told a story of chastity, it would be difficult to use this as evidence of a widely agreed-upon social value. But because numerous authors described the social importance of sexual morality and its relationship to divine favor, the historian can piece together elements of the social fabric and understand something about gender expectations.

Inscriptions

Recognizing the limited information available from the writings of elite men, scholars turned to other kinds of sources to supplement their knowledge of women.[19] Inscriptions were carved in stone to commemorate an important event, publicly thank a benefactor, or honor the dead. There was a large increase in public statues and building projects in the first century, and as a result many inscriptions remain. These sources provide information that supplements the literary material.

The evidence of inscriptions presents its own set of difficulties. Wealthier people more likely could afford to purchase a building, statue, inscription, or other object that survives. Yet the relative prosperity of the first and second centuries allowed many people of more modest means to produce inscriptions for the deceased or to honor leaders of their religious groups and civic associations. Inscriptions represented a wider segment of the population than were described in philosophical writings but still tell us little about the lives of the poorest classes.

Another problem is that inscriptions were meant to honor a patron or deceased relative. As such, they often gave an idealized version of that person rather than a realistic portrait. For example, many funerary inscriptions described the family connections of the deceased and praised him or her for virtuous behavior. One such inscription was dedicated to Amymone in the first century B.C.E.: "Here lies Amymone, wife of Marcus, best and most beautiful, a worker in wool, pious, chaste, thrifty, faithful, a stayer at home" (*ILS* 8402). In this case, the reader learns little of Amymone's family—only that she was married to Marcus. She was honored with a long list of traditional female virtues. Taken together, the list portrayed Amymone as the ideal wife. Because of this, it is hard to say whether the attributes provided an accurate description of Amymone or simply characterized her as a virtuous person.

Funerary inscriptions on tombs or caskets sometimes included pictures, which depicted men and women of varying means as they wished to be remembered. One image that survives is that of a potter and his wife (see figure 1.1). The relief shows the potter seated on the right, posed at work making a cup. His spouse, on

FIGURE 1.1 Funerary Relief for Potter's Family. Virginia Museum of Fine Arts, Richmond. Adolph D. and Wilkins C. Williams Fund. Photo: Katherine Wetzel. Used by permission.

the left, has a domestic pose. She sits in a high-backed chair rather than on a work stool, and her hair is elaborately dressed in the style of the day.

Interpreters ask whether such an image was realistic or idealized. A pre-industrial economy needed all adults to contribute to the household. At the potter's income level, the economic demands of the family were unlikely to leave time and money for the elaborate hairstyle and leisure represented in the picture. Instead of providing a realistic portrait, the woman's seated pose and domestic objects honored her as a respectable matron.

Like the literary sources discussed above, these inscriptions also had persuasive aims and cannot be taken at face value as a window into these women's lives. The attributes in Amymone's funeral epitaph represented an idealized version of feminine virtue. Take, for example, the final trait her husband listed: a "stayer at home" (*domiseda*). Women were often described in antiquity as ideally occupied within the home. In another example from a literary source, the first-century Jewish author Philo wrote, "Women are best suited to the indoor life, which never strays from the house" (*Leg.* 3.169). Amymone is portrayed as attaining such virtue. But there is little evidence that women were confined or chose to stay within their homes. Lower-class women were likely to have lived in homes that adjoined a courtyard where much of the household work was done. They may have lived in or above the shops where they worked alongside their husbands in business. The term *domiseda* seems more likely to have communicated Amymone's devotion to the needs of her household rather than her actual location. During her lifetime, her work likely took her outside their living quarters.

In a similar vein, the images in relief carvings depicted those commemorated in an idealized rather than a realistic form. Like Amymone's attributes, the pose of the woman in figure 1.1 conveyed her devotion to the household. Her hairstyle and posture portrayed her as a modest Roman matron.[20] The virtue depicted does not tell us how the woman lived her life. But it does give us insight into the gendered virtues that the monument's inscriber assumed its viewers shared. By erecting such monuments, Romans displayed their status. The artifacts help us to see the virtues people wanted to project and the visual shorthand they used to encapsulate those qualities.

Interpreters look for patterns across these sources. It is difficult to interpret a single inscription without having other knowledge of the context that produced it. The image of the potter was not the only one of its kind. Another image of a butcher's shop (see figure 1.2) portrayed a husband and wife in similar poses: he is at work on the right; she is seated in a dignified pose. The repetition in the two works points to shared values that these images depicted. Both images also corresponded to the virtues stated in Amymone's inscription. Taken together, the inscriptions give us insight into agreed-upon social norms.

Papyri

Papyrus records and letters give a more realistic, if partial, view of ancient people's lives. These documents were often tools for communicating information of a practical nature rather than for

FIGURE 1.2 Funerary Relief for Butcher's Family. Skulpturensammlung, Staatliche Kunstsammlungen, Dresden, Germany. Photo: Elke Estel. Art Resource, NY. Used by permission.

asserting one's opinion or status. Because of this, these records provide information that the literary sources do not.

Papyri often recorded everyday economic transactions. For example, records from a village in Egypt showed women selling and registering ownership of camels, a primary source of income in that location (*P.Grenf.* 2.45a; *M.Chr.* 260). Although little is known about the women, the papyri suggested that there was nothing unusual about women owning such property. They expressed economic transactions of men and women in similar terms. Women appeared less frequently than men in these sources, but they undertook similar kinds of activities.

Interpreting inscriptions and papyri still requires attention to the context and rhetorical aims of the writing. For example, in one papyrus, Demetria, an Alexandrian woman living in Oxyrhynchos (in Egypt), appointed her grandson as her legal representative. She wrote that she was "unable to attend the court by reason of womanly frailty" (*P.Oxy.* 2.261).[21] The statement reflected a cultural assumption that women were frail by nature. Yet the claim of frailty as a quality of women lies in some tension with the rest of the document. Demetria directed that "she has appointed her aforesaid grandson Chairemon as her legal representative before every authority and every court, with the same powers as she, Demetria, who has appointed him, would have had if present, for she consents to this appointment. The contract is authoritative." The language of the document suggested that Demetria expected to have some "powers" before the court, powers that she transmitted to her grandson. Demetria mentioned a guardian in the same document but did not name him as her legal representative, choosing instead her grandson, Chairemon. Demetria's claim of "frailty" drew on assumptions about women to explain her absence in court. Yet it also appeared in some tension with her actions to secure her legal interests. As with the literary works and inscriptions, papyri also require thoughtful consideration of the purposes and context of the writing.

CONCLUSION

This availability of increased numbers of inscriptions and papyri has changed the kinds of evidence available. Papyri give us a more mundane and less idealized view of life. As such, they show women's participation in economic and legal decision making. The everyday nature of these transactions gives a picture of people's lives that is unaddressed by most literary sources. Inscriptions give an idealized view but also praise women for being in positions of authority and honor. These are the kinds of positions that seem to be expressly forbidden in the philosophical and legal materials.

The new evidence from inscriptions and papyri intensifies the questions that already existed in the literary sources. It is common to see women being praised for their leadership and patronage of cities and community groups. Women managed farms, bequeathed property, and arranged apprenticeships. They were teachers, priests, and magistrates.

The variety of kinds of evidence and the conflicting signals of these sources raise questions of interpretation. How should a modern reader understand statements of women's inferiority or limitations alongside other evidence celebrating women's prominent roles? The next chapter discusses the ways that historians have assessed the conflicting evidence and explains the approach of this book.

Chapters 3 through 7 each focus on an aspect of women's lives in the New Testament period. I present evidence for gendered virtues, practices of marriage and divorce, the importance of class status, the occupations of women, and their speech and silence. In each case, I try to give a full description of the kinds of evidence available and to draw conclusions about the ways women participated in that element of communal life.

Each chapter also ends with a brief discussion of New Testament texts. In these sections I consider passages of the New Testament in light of the chapter to see what new possibilities for interpretation may emerge. Readers should not expect that the historical information offered in the chapter will "solve" once and for all the question of interpretation that the biblical texts raise. Texts always have more than one possible good interpretation, and the history of biblical interpretation confirms that many interpretations are possible. My hope is not to answer all the questions related to the New Testament texts but to allow new observations and interpretations to emerge.

Chapter 2

Interpreting Evidence
for Women's Lives

READERS OF THE NEW TESTAMENT often share an impression that ancient women's lives were highly restricted. Men led and women were expected to follow. Men owned property and women relied on them for support. Men pursued honor and women tried to avoid shame. People expected men to be active and courageous and to excel in a variety of careers, but they valued women only for their virginity (as girls) and their capacity for childbearing (as adults).

Some of the evidence for women's lives in the first and second centuries supports the impressions stated above. For example, the first century Jewish philosopher, Philo of Alexandria, wrote, "The women are best suited to the indoor life which never strays from the house. . . . A woman, then, should not be a busybody, meddling with matters outside her household concerns, but should seek a life of seclusion. She should not show herself off like a vagrant in the streets before the eyes of other men, except when she has to go to the temple" (*Spec.* 3.169–170).[1] Philo's view confined women's activities to a narrow arena.

Women could also be criticized for being immodest, idle, or outspoken. For example, the Roman author Juvenal presented a satirical portrait of a learned, elite woman who spoke with too much authority: "But she's much worse, the woman who as soon as she's taken her place at dinner is praising Virgil and forgiving Elissa on her deathbed, who pits the poets against one another and assesses them. . . . The schoolteachers give way, the teachers of rhetoric are beaten, the whole party falls silent, there'll not be a word from any lawyer or auctioneer—not even from another woman." (*Sat.* 6.434–440).[2] Juvenal painted a picture in which such women absurdly overstepped the bounds of decency. His words represented some of the social norms of his day, in which women rightly deferred to men of the same social class.

There is a good deal of evidence, however, that women exercised a surprising degree of political and social influence in this period— certainly greater than in many cultures before or since. Consider Agusia Priscilla, who was honored with an inscription and statue decreed by her city. The inscription honored Priscilla for expenses incurred as a priestess of Spes and Salus Augusta, and stated that her gifts were inspired "by the example of illustrious women." She refurbished the portico of the temple with her own money and gave shows to honor the emperor. Pleased with the honor, she repaid the cost of the statue herself (*CIL* 14.2804 [*ILS* 6218]). This inscription is one example of many women honored in similar ways for their provision of services and building projects undertaken for the benefit of the community. The actions represented here are not what modern readers would expect from sources like Philo and Juvenal. While Philo asserted the norm of female modesty and seclusion and Juvenal was critical of women's speech, Agusia Priscilla's inscription and many others like it offered public praise of women for their acts of civic leadership.

These conflicting signals are repeated over and over in the evidence that remains from the New Testament period. A good deal of evidence suggested that women were expected to be quiet and submissive. At the same time, evidence also showed women performing a wide range of tasks. Agusia Priscilla's actions were not an anomaly but fit within the cultural norms I describe in chapters 3 through 6. Many women of this period owned property, ran businesses, served as civic and religious officials, and pursued the social interests of their families.

Thus, the evidence for women's capacities to act yields mixed results. One task of this book is to bring to light the more active roles that women played in their communities, because this evidence contradicts the assumptions that many modern readers have. If we read the New Testament alongside only writers like Philo and Juvenal, we will have a distorted picture indeed. However, the larger task of this book is to understand how the varied evidence fits together. How did it make sense that women were praised both for modesty and for civic leadership? How did ideals of subordination make sense alongside women's active leadership? In this chapter, I consider a number of ways scholars have answered these questions and describe the approach of this book.

EXPLAINING DIVERSE EVIDENCE

The diversity in the existing evidence has long been noted by scholars, who explained this variety in a number of ways. In this section I review some of the popular explanations. Earlier scholars dismissed the evidence for women's leadership by suggesting that their titles were merely honorific. Some recent scholarship instead presented women's leadership as real but exceptional. Other scholars asserted that women's leadership was only possible in certain communities, or they assigned female leadership to the private sphere. I argue that none of these theories explains the evidence available for women's roles. Understanding why these explanations do not work sets the foundation for a new approach to interpreting the conflicting evidence.

Women Leaders Were Not "Real" Leaders

One type of reasoning regarding the conflicting evidence for the roles of women explained away the evidence of women's active leadership. In this view, women leaders were not "real" leaders. Their titles or roles had no real authority and thus should be discounted. For example, scholars have often acknowledged the titles attributed to women in inscriptions, where they were recognized as priests and magistrates of cities. Yet some concluded these titles were "simply honorary," meaning that the office holder did not exercise any power or function but simply held a title. For example, writing in 1940, A. H. M. Jones admitted that Greek women held magistracies but described their positions as "those of a more ornamental character."[3] Scholars like Jones implied that women office holders had no power.

This line of reasoning fails to consider the changing nature of political power during the Imperial period. At the end of the Republican period, women were already involved in politics through the exercise of social influence. Although they did not vote or hold membership in the senate, they exercised power through other political channels, especially through family ties and patronage.[4] Social networks were important avenues through which to assert political power in this period, and they were available to women as well as men.

The argument that women's titles were "merely honorary" also neglects the importance of honor within Mediterranean cultures of the time. The pursuit of honor was a motivating force within society and was a primary reason people sought out religious and civic offices. The patron used his or her wealth and political influence on behalf of the city, and the appropriate response for the people of the city was to honor the patron. (See the discussion of patronage in chapter 5.) Inscriptions that honored male or female office holders and donors were one tangible form of honor. Cities or civic groups offered to honor a generous donor by erecting a statue in a prominent place, proclaiming that person's importance through the visual representation of the statue and the publication of the decree that authorized it. As Ramsay MacMullen argued, for both men and women, "Surely the heart of the matter . . . was the deference secured forever from one's fellow citizens through one's being, for only a day or for only a few days a year, at the head of the parade, or in front of crowds, and thereafter known by a new title and memorialized in stone in the forum."[5] To say that an office was "merely honorary" is anachronistic because honor was a form of cultural capital that could translate into social and political power. Women pursued honor alongside their male peers.[6]

Interpreters of early Christian texts have also minimized the leadership of women seen in these sources. Many have read the restrictive language in some New Testament passages as canceling out the evidence of women's leadership. For example, writing on the qualifications of women deacons in 1 Tim 3:11, Jouette Bassler asserted that the letter's instruction that women should not teach or have authority over men restricted the actions of women deacons (1 Tim 2:12). She wrote: "The text gives no indication of the responsibilities of these women, though the injunctions in 2:12 would seem to preclude any real leadership role."[7] This interpretation claimed that the ideals limiting speech always governed the actions of deacons and thereby prevented "real" leadership by women. Like some of the studies of non-Christian women, this approach assumed that conventional virtues precluded meaningful action by women.

Women Leaders Were Exceptions to the Rule

Another strategy in interpreting the contradictory evidence for women's roles has been to argue that the few women leaders were exceptions to the rule. Unusual circumstances allowed women to subvert the rules that governed social action and to take on leadership roles. The rule of subordination to men continued to apply to all other women, but a few were released from strict observation.

Some scholars have assumed that females exercised leadership only when no male was available to play the role. This explanation bypasses evidence of married women honored for substantive civic roles. Inscriptions do not always mention the donor's marital status, but sometimes enough information is given to confirm that the woman had a living husband or son. One example is Junia Rustica, a married woman who was generous to her city and also provided statues for her husband and son (see chapter 7). Therefore, a better explanation is needed to account for the available evidence.

Other scholars argued that only extremely wealthy, elite women held leadership roles.[8] Such occurrences were not part of the regular cultural landscape, and so they did not affect most women's lives, which continued to be dominated by men. This explanation fits somewhat better with the available evidence because the kind of patronage honored with statues and civic inscriptions required large outlays of money. Wealthy women were most likely to attain such durable honors.

Yet to view such women as "exceptions to the rule" is still problematic for two reasons. One is the large number of women patrons visible in the evidence. Inscriptions celebrating men outnumbered those for women. Yet women were also honored, and the frequency with which they appear in the evidence suggests that they contributed regularly to their cities and towns as patrons. Instead of viewing each instance of women's patronage as exceptional, it makes more sense to consider social norms that supported their participation. The second reason is that the evidence of women's patronage is not limited to elite women. Women of humbler means acted as patrons by making loans or giving smaller gifts to their communities (see chapter 5). Evidence of elite patronage is more likely to have survived, but there is enough evidence of patronage by nonelite women to suggest a wider social basis that supported their actions.

Explaining women's leadership as "exceptional" made more sense before scholars of the last forty years brought to light a good deal of evidence for the participation of women in civic and religious life. Instead of seeing these women as exceptional, scholars today tend to reframe the way the rules were understood to account for the regular participation of women. I take up this task of reframing at the end of this chapter.

Women's Leadership Was Limited to Distinct Communities

Scholars of early Christianity have also explained the conflicting evidence as an indication that some communities allowed women's leadership while others did not. What has come to be the consensus position emerged in the 1970s and '80s when feminist scholars mounted an argument for the leadership of women in the earliest churches. Many argued that women acted as leaders in the earliest churches, but their leadership was eliminated over time, especially as the church began to take on more structured institutional forms. One pioneer of this argument was Elisabeth Schüssler Fiorenza, whose work *In Memory of Her* is now a classic in the field. She argued, for example, that the language in 1 Timothy forbidding women from teaching or having authority over men (1 Tim 2:11–12) represented one community that limited women's teaching. The letter was composed in response to other Christians who encouraged women to speak.[9] Another pioneer in this research was Elaine Pagels, who argued that Gnostic Christians allowed women's leadership while proto-orthodox Christians did not.[10]

Some scholars have divided not only Christian groups but also the society as a whole into groups that disagreed about women's roles. In a more recent example, Bruce Winter traced the emergence of the "new Roman woman" through factors like rising property ownership and civic titles, trends I discuss in chapters 4 and 5. Winter argued that a group he identified as the avant-garde supported this social trend. Others, including the emperor Augustus, opposed their behavior.[11] Winter's approach assigned the conflicting evidence to different groups within Roman society at large. He went on to apply this social background to the New Testament language restricting women's speech and encouraging modesty, arguing that it was a reaction against these "new women."

Scholars of early Christianity have also explained the varying evidence for women's participation by dividing it into groups corresponding to the marital status of the women involved. A common argument has been that Christian women gained autonomy by rejecting marriage and pursuing a celibate lifestyle. Women in celibate groups took on roles as leaders of their communities. The value of sexual self-control is visible in the New Testament, where Paul preferred remaining unmarried to marriage because it was evidence of self-control (1 Cor 7:1–9). Many interpreters have seen Paul's option not to marry, when practiced by women, as something that gave women a means to escape the control of men.[12]

Some recent scholarship has tempered the idea that celibate women escaped male control. Elizabeth Castelli, for example, argued that the life of virginity also restricted women's lives, though perhaps in different ways than marriage did.[13] However, many scholars have still repeated the idea that celibate women gained freedom. For example, Ross Kraemer wrote, "Real celibate women escaped to some extent an underlying ideological system of gender relations that subordinates women to men."[14] The idea is that these women leaders stood somehow outside of the cultural norms that applied to marriage.

Dividing women's participation into distinct groups would be more compelling if the evidence itself were easily divisible in this fashion. Instead, much of the evidence for women's participation mixes the restrictive ideals of feminine behavior with women's action. Numerous inscriptions praise women's leadership and patronage alongside feminine virtues like modesty (see chapters 3 and 5). The philosopher Plutarch reiterated women's inherent inferiority to men, but he also praised women for their political and military acumen. The jurist Gaius acknowledged women's guardianship as a legal norm based on the inherent weakness of women while admitting he saw no reason for the practice in his day. It is difficult to account for such evidence with distinct social groups. The approach I describe in this chapter makes room for the possibility of complex or conflicting views within a single source or community.

Women's Leadership Was Limited to the Private Sphere

Another explanation of the diverse evidence has been to define women's leadership as something restricted to the private sphere. The idea is that women had substantial authority within the home but were restricted from public roles. There is ample evidence that associated virtuous women with the work of the household. The quotation from Philo at the beginning of this chapter is one example: "Women are best suited to the indoor life, which never strays from the house." In the light of such statements, many historians have concluded that women's leadership was restricted to "private" roles.

Although this argument was popular among classicists as well as historians of early Christianity, it has been especially persuasive in interpretations of the Christian texts because of the prevalence of house churches in the early church. Many early Christian communities met in members' houses, and this location was conducive to women's leadership.[15] Scholars argued that when churches developed into institutional forms outside of houses, women's leadership was eliminated because they could not lead in public.

However, modern definitions of public and private differ so much from ancient conceptions that the terms are confusing rather than helpful. Readers today are likely to imagine the "public sphere" as a wide arena that includes things like business, education, and the use of political influence. However, in the Roman world, "public" life included a narrow range of activities, especially legislative and judicial functions.[16] These functions were the purview of elite men and thus were off limits to many men as well as to women. This was especially true in the Imperial period, when the concentration of political power in the emperor made him the sole "public" person.[17]

While the public arena was a narrower realm than modern readers commonly imagine, a wide range of activities were classified as "private" concerns. As Kate Cooper has argued, "Romans drew the distinction between 'the public' and 'the private' . . . in terms of proprietary interest. This meant that production and commerce fell, along with the household, on the 'private' side of the divide."[18] The household was the center of production in the ancient world and women participated actively both as laborers and as managers of production. Women's household work also regularly carried them outside of the house into the market and shops. Some women worked alongside their husbands in business.[19] Modern scholars might naturally imagine this participation to be "public" and therefore part of what women were expected to avoid. But it seems more accurate to say that production and commerce belonged to the realm of the household and were therefore appropriate to women.

Similarly, much of the social influence exerted through patronage also belonged to the realm of the household. As Harriet Fertik wrote, "The house served not as a retreat but as a setting for social and political activity."[20] The household was a meeting place both for social peers and for patron and client.[21] Women played important roles hosting social events and exercising influence with peers, patrons, and clients.

Architecturally, houses also blurred the line between public and private. The spaces of elite households usually had multiple uses: the room that received visitors in the morning might become a workspace in the daytime. In small houses, household labor was often performed in a shared courtyard.[22] The household domain included a wide range of activities, many of which would be categorized today as "public."

Private interests impinged on "public" spaces as well. In a recent book, classicist Amy Russell argued that the Roman Forum was political space that mixed public and private interests. It was a market and busy thoroughfare, and thus it was "public" in the sense of being accessible. But because it was political space, elite citizens competed with one another to mark it as their own. Through statues and buildings that bore their names, citizens mingled their private interests with the public uses of the Forum. In the Roman period, the civic spaces in provincial cities were used in similar ways. Populated with statues and bordered with buildings built by wealthy donors, the streets and squares presented a mix of private as well as civic or political interests. Women competed for honor alongside men by donating statues and buildings (see chapter 5).

In the end, it seems better to discard the words public and private because they obscure more than they illuminate. I am interested in describing things like social influence, political advocacy, economic activity, and civic offices of women. Categorizing these actions as public or private is not a primary concern. For these reasons I avoid the use of these words and try instead to describe the content of women's speech and actions.

THE APPROACH OF THIS BOOK

This book offers an alternative explanation of the evidence for women's lives. Greek and Roman cultures included norms for women's behavior that were multiple and conflicting. Some of these norms required women to remain at home, submit to their husband's authority, and remain silent. But others encouraged women to pursue the interests of their families and communities, activities that required participation in economic and social life. Actors within the culture understood what it meant to abide by these complex social norms.

In this section I offer two ways of understanding how the evidence that seems contradictory to us may have made sense within its ancient context. First, I describe how contemporary understandings of culture make room for the idea that conflicting norms exist within cultures. Cultures provide a set of rules that shape behavior, but these rules are inhabited in multiple ways. Furthermore, actors within cultures negotiate the tensions between existing norms. Second, I describe one cultural pattern in the Imperial period where feminine norms of behavior overlapped with ideals of civic leadership. These cultural trends supported the increased participation of women.

Multiple and Conflicting Cultural Norms

One of the reasons it makes sense to reassess the ancient evidence now is that our understanding of culture has changed.[23] The view of women as exceptions to the rule implies an understanding in which culture provides a set of rules for individuals to follow. When the rules are broken, either an exception is made or a new social group is formed in opposition to the dominant culture.

More recent social theory challenges this idea and tries to account for more of the complexity and change that occurs within cultures. One important idea is that culture provides a sense not only of what the rules are but also of how they should be applied under different circumstances. For example, modern American culture has norms of modesty, though they differ considerably from the ancient norms discussed in the next chapter. But even within American culture, modesty is not a single rule that applies equally to all situations. It means one thing to dress modestly at the beach, and another thing entirely to dress modestly in church. People who are reared within the culture are not likely to confuse the two situations. Culture provides standards of modesty and the social understanding required to live by the rules of culture.[24]

Moreover, the rules of culture are constantly negotiated and often in conflict. As Michel de Certeau argued, "Each individual is a locus in which an incoherent (and often contradictory) plurality of such relational determinations interact."[25] Because of this variety, individuals necessarily make choices about how to inhabit cultural norms and roles. Even clearly stated dispositions like modesty or the subordination of women do not exist in a vacuum but interact with other cultural norms and expectations.

Instead of seeing culture as a coherent force scripting human action, individuals may be understood to function with what Ann Swidler has called a "cultural repertoire."[26] Cultures provide an array of social roles, values, and ways of making meaning, which actors employ, depending on the resources and power available to them. The dispositions of culture shape human action, but they allow for multiple expressions of the same value and even, to some extent, choice between values.

Furthermore, as new situations arise, actors may employ practices associated with one role in new arenas.[27] For example, scholars have long studied the relationship between voluntary associations in Greco-Roman cultures and the organizational structure of synagogues and churches. Titles and roles that were familiar in civic and voluntary associations migrated into other realms like the synagogue and the church.[28] In a similar fashion, scholars have looked for roles that were already available to women, arguing that they held similar positions in the church.[29] Cultural innovation, such as a new religious group, emerges within a culture and reconfigures existing norms and practices.

With this understanding of culture in mind, interpreters might expect to find ancient evidence expressing complex and even conflicting values. The differences interpreters have noticed in the evidence may not define boundaries between discrete groups, each with a different perspective on women and gender. Instead, this variety may indicate that complex cultural norms are at work within one individual or social group.

Understanding culture from this perspective changes some of the questions interpreters may ask of these texts. Interpreters who encounter social norms like the expectation of women's modesty may ask what modesty looked like in practice. Instead of viewing women leaders as exceptions to the patriarchal rule, interpreters might wonder what cultural forces gave rise to diverse expressions of gendered norms. How did rules of culture allow such "exceptions" to arise? (Or, given the large number of "exceptional" women in antiquity, what rules better account for the diverse evidence available?) What does the conflicting evidence for women's leadership and submission tell us about the dispositions of culture?

Gendered Virtues and Civic Participation

Interpreting the evidence for women's participation in Roman society involves looking for ways the tensions would have made sense to the people of the time. One pattern in this period was the use of domestic virtues as civic attributes. Virtues that were associated with traditional household roles came to be used to express the duty of citizens to their city. This trend helps explain support for women's civic participation. The overlap between household and civic virtue is one way to understand how women's leadership was consistent with other cultural norms.

In the Imperial period, domestic attributes became the core of a new civic vocabulary.[30] The shift to rule by an emperor was a major social and political change at the end of the first century B.C.E. Decisions that were formerly shared among an elite group of men were concentrated in the hands of the emperor. This change was sustained in part by renewed attention to the connections between domestic ideals and civic responsibility. The elevation of virtues like loyalty to one's spouse and the wise use of resources for the good of the whole helped to mobilize people's private interests for the good of the state. Because society already valued these virtues in women, the public discourse made additional space for women's participation in the civic realm.

Legal changes early in the empire made household behavior a matter of civic concern. For example, Augustus enacted marriage laws that gave incentives for citizens to marry and to remarry when widowed or divorced. At the same time, the laws made adultery a crime rather than a family matter. Similarly, a new right called the *ius liberorum* made the production of citizens a matter of honor that brought concrete benefits. Under this law, freeborn men with three children had preference in appointments to certain offices. Women with the right could conduct their business without the consent of a guardian. The same status was available to freedwomen with four children. (For more on these legal changes, see chapter 4.) Such legal changes made marriage and childbearing matters of civic responsibility, and they rewarded both male and female citizens who contributed in this way to the public good.

At the same time, the emperor made domestic virtues part of his public image. Kristina Milnor noted, "Augustus sought systematically to characterize himself and his household through a performance of traditional Roman domesticity."[31] Suetonius gave considerable attention to the emperor's family life and virtues (*Aug.* 61–73). Augustus's autobiography emphasized his modesty and the influence of his mother as a way of underscoring the emperor's relationship to the household.[32] He presented himself as a person who valued and was formed by traditional family virtues.

Many scholars have seen the emphasis on domestic virtues as repressive of women. The subordination of women to their husbands served the interests of the state as well as the family. The emphasis on marriage and childbearing put pressure on women to conform to traditional roles and remain subordinate to men. For example, regarding Plutarch's *Advice to the Bride and Groom*, Jo Ann McNamara wrote, "In considering the dynamics of a couple, they were seeking readjustments in the gender system that would persuade potentially rebellious women to accept its strictures."[33] From this perspective, the promotion of domestic virtues restricted women's freedom and maintained male control.

Without denying the limitations placed on women, recent scholars have emphasized the effects of these trends to carve out space for women within civic discourse. Such arguments try to account for the wide use of domestic virtues to characterize both men and women, as well as the body of evidence praising women for civic leadership. Beth Severy argued that the Augustan marriage laws "officially made family behavior part of a citizen's duty. . . . One's family responsibilities thus became primary duties to the community."[34] As domesticity took on importance even for the emperor as proof of civic responsibility, women's virtues also began to appear as achievements for the good of the city or state.

The empress Livia is another example of the role domestic virtues came to play in the civic realm. Livia characterized herself with traditional feminine virtues at the same time she embraced a civic role. Severy argued, "Livia used her association with Augustus and the rising importance of family roles in official rhetoric to create a public status out of exemplary domesticity."[35] One of Livia's civic acts was the dedication of a shrine to Concordia. *Concordia* was both a quality describing ideal marital relationships and a goddess Romans appealed to in times of political strife. Livia's association with this shrine evoked political virtues at the same time it contributed to the idealization of the emperor's family life. Livia also restored the temple of Fortuna Muliebris, the site of a cult honoring the patriotism of two women who acted to prevent an attack on the city.[36] Through the restoration, Livia displayed her devotion to the gods, and in doing so she represented traditional virtues. She also evoked the precedent of two honorable women who worked on behalf of the state.

Even as she undertook these political acts, Livia was characterized with the traditional female virtues that are the subject of the next chapter. Suetonius portrayed Livia, along with Octavia and Julia, as making Augustus's clothing (Suetonius, *Aug.* 73). Being "a worker in wool" was an iconic image of the loyal, industrious, and modest wife. Although the scope of Livia's labor was likely exaggerated, the rhetorical goal was to associate the imperial women with the traditional domestic labor of wool-working.[37] Other writers of the period described Livia's *pudicitia* (sexual virtue or modesty). Ovid, encouraging his wife to seek Livia's favor, said that Livia "by her virtue gives surety that the olden time conquers not our age in praise of chastity (*pudicitia*)" (*Pont.* 3.1.114–116).[38] Although aware of her political influence, such authors acclaimed Livia's modesty as a way of asserting her virtue.

Livia was a woman with exceptional power, but she was not "the exception to the rule" by which women were otherwise powerless and invisible. The social norms Livia invoked had a broad social appeal and were encouraged as the basis of civic benefaction. Instead of stepping outside the norm, Livia publicized these conventions that sustained communal interests in the absence of participatory government. Livia was frequently cited as an emblem of matronly virtue and lifted up for others to follow, as I discuss in chapter 5. The civic discourse employed by Augustus and Livia drew on existing concepts and vocabulary and expanded their role in the civic arena.

CONCLUSION

In this book I interpret the conflicting reports about women's leadership as evidence of complex social norms and practices. From a modern perspective, the position of women in first-century culture is paradoxical: at the same time that women were ideally described as modest and confined to the home, some virtues required women to exercise leadership and to pursue the broad interests of their households and cities. The evidence for this paradox is not new, and many scholars have pointed to the seeming contradictions. In chapter 3, I describe how actions that appear contradictory to us may have fit within the cultural norms of the time. Women were expected to exhibit the virtues of modesty, industry, and loyalty to family. However, women from various circumstances negotiated and embodied these virtues in a variety of culturally acceptable ways. Inhabiting these virtues led women to embrace a wide variety of social and familial roles. Developments of the first century supported the appearance of women in leadership roles because domestic virtues took on added importance as evidence of civic responsibility.

This more complex view of the cultural norms for women's behavior points to a new way of understanding the varieties in the evidence for women's participation in early Christian communities. Viewed as part of a cultural repertoire, women who inhabited leadership roles did not step outside of culture, evading norms of women's modesty. Instead, they applied the norms regarding modesty in combination with other culturally available roles and norms. The different roles that women played in antiquity did not define the boundaries between communities with different gender ideologies. The possibility for different roles and leadership by women existed within and across various subgroups in the New Testament world.

Chapter 3

Gendered Virtues

THE LIFE CIRCUMSTANCES OF INDIVIDUAL women varied significantly due to diverse local, social, and legal practices of the period. However, there was also widespread agreement on the ideal qualities of the virtuous woman. Across the centuries and from numerous locations, different kinds of sources portrayed the ideal woman as modest, industrious, and loyal to her family. There were various ways to express these virtues, but the ideals themselves were remarkably consistent.

Instead of assuming a single way in which women were virtuous in antiquity, this book explores what the virtues looked like in a particular time and place. When women were praised for modesty, what kinds of things were they doing? How did other virtues like industry and loyalty intersect with and complicate expressions of modesty? This chapter describes evidence from a variety of sources in the first century B.C.E. through second century C.E. that displayed traditional feminine virtues. In exploring this evidence, I look for ways that the descriptions of a woman and her actions can both fit and complicate the view that feminine virtues were restrictive.

The qualities of modesty, industry, and loyalty overlapped in significant ways, as I discuss further below. Although I address each virtue individually, it is difficult to separate these ideals. The interaction between the virtues makes them more difficult to describe in isolation, but it also explains some of the complexity in the ways the virtues appear in the ancient evidence. A woman who was modest might have been ideally depicted as remaining at home. However, the same woman's loyalty to her family might have led her out of the home as she sought to meet the needs of her household. The interplay between the virtues suggests that women engaged in a wide variety of activities. Moreover, as they did so, they were not seen as "breaking the rules" of feminine virtue. Instead, women inhabited these norms in a variety of ways that the culture affirmed.

MODESTY

Modesty was a complex virtue in antiquity. Some meanings were similar to what we might think of as modesty today. For example, one traditional expression of modesty for women was covering their bodies. In an earlier period, Greek women wrapped their bodies and covered their heads in layers of cloth. Plutarch wrote this anecdote of a female philosopher six centuries earlier: "Theano once exposed her hand as she was arranging her cloak. 'What a beautiful arm,' said someone. 'But not public property,' she replied" (*Conj. praec.* 31).[1] Plutarch's story expressed the ideal of modesty through covering the body.

But in the first and second centuries, modesty in dress more often meant simple (as opposed to lavish) attire. This was a period of prosperity for many people, and with that prosperity came the ability to display one's wealth through jewelry, expensive fabrics, and elaborate hairstyles. The image of the woman in figure 3.1 exemplifies one of the hairstyles that became popular among elite women in this period. Styling one's hair in this way required a great deal of effort and often a household slave whose time could be devoted to such a project. Because of this, it was not only a fashion statement but also a display of wealth.

Such displays were an important element of a family's exhibition of social status. Wealthy families gained honor and prestige through their use and display of wealth. Hosting dinner parties, appearing in public with slaves in tow, and wearing expensive clothing or jewelry contributed to the construction of the family's social image within the community.

FIGURE 3.1 Portrait of a Priestess. © Michael C. Carlos Museum, Emory University. Photo: Bruce M. White, 2010. Used by permission.

However, the ancient sources also displayed awareness that such extravagance could conflict with other important social values. Plutarch provided an example of a military leader, Lysander: "The tyrant of Sicily sent expensive cloaks and necklaces to Lysander's daughters. Lysander refused them, saying, 'These ornaments will disfigure me more than they will adorn my daughters'" (*Conj. praec.* 26). Lysander understood his own status to be connected to what his daughters wore. Although the gifts would assert the family's social status, he decided that they would "disfigure" him by connecting him with a tyrant. He chose to reject the gifts. Modesty as a virtue could compete with the value of displaying one's social status through dress and ornamentation.

Plutarch's advice on the adornment of women pointed to a similarity between restraint in dress and the judgment required of leaders. Plutarch's example of Lysander was part of a longer teaching in which he upheld modest dress for women: "Sophocles anticipated Lysander's thought: 'there's no adornment here to see, you wretch, but lack of adornment, and your heart's blind folly.' 'Adornment,' said Crates, 'is what adorns'; and what adorns a woman is what makes her better ordered—not gold nor emerald nor scarlet, but whatever gives an impression of dignity, discipline, and modesty" (*Conj. praec.* 26). Instead of elaborate dress, women could be metaphorically adorned with virtue. The playwright Sophocles and the philosopher Crates added their authority to Plutarch's argument. By refusing lavish gifts from a tyrannical ruler, Lysander displayed good judgment. Modest dress required similar self-discipline, and thus displayed one's virtue.

The idea of order and discipline in the quote above was at the heart of what it meant to be modest in antiquity. The Greek word *sōphrosunē* or modesty also meant "self-control." Its opposite was *akolasia*, "self-indulgence." The *sōphrōn*—the wise or self-controlled person—prioritized the needs of the household or city over his or her own pleasures. Sōphrosunē was both a male and a female virtue. Although modesty looked different for men than for women, the emphasis on self-control was the same. Because lavish dress could divert household resources, simple dress indicated self-control. It expressed wise judgment about the use of communal resources.

Another expression of modesty was careful speech. Philosophers wrote prolifically about the difficulty and importance of controlling the tongue. "For silence is a wise thing, and better than any speech. . . . The words unspoken can easily be uttered later; but the spoken word cannot possibly be recalled" (Pseudo-Plutarch, *Lib. ed.* 14).[2] The ability to speak openly and boldly was prized, especially among friends. But silence was also an important virtue and was seen as difficult to achieve.

Because Roman society was highly stratified, knowing whom one could speak to and what to say was very important. Plutarch wrote, "It will also be very advantageous for chatterers to frequent invariably the company of their superiors and elders, out of respect for whose opinion they will become accustomed to silence" (*Garr.* 23).[3] Silence in the presence of one's social superiors expressed self-control and acknowledged the honor due the person of higher rank.

Social rank was a complex calculation that included more than simply one's wealth or class status. Respect was also due to people based on their age, gender, citizenship, and family of origin (see also chapter 5). So, in the quote above, the young person was expected to be silent in the presence of adults because an older person from a similar class background had higher status. The quote implied that the young person would be expected to speak in other contexts; but because of the relative honor due the elderly he should practice self-control in their presence.

Similarly, women were of lower social rank than men. When other factors were equal, men had greater status than women. Like the youth in the presence of the elderly, women's silence among their male peers was a virtue because it acknowledged the relatively higher rank accorded to the men. Thus, silence among women was another expression of modesty or self-control. Plutarch used his anecdote about Theano, quoted above, to assert the importance of modest speech, not modest dress: "Not only the arms but the words of a modest woman (*sōphrōn*) must never be public property. She should be shy with her speech as with her body, and guard it against strangers. Feelings, character, and disposition can all be seen in a woman's talk" (*Conj. praec.* 31). Plutarch's words conveyed the idea that women can and should speak. He advised that silence in certain contexts conveyed one's virtue.

Not all women were viewed as inferior to all men, however. Women with greater wealth or excellent lineage had higher status than men from humbler origins. In some contexts, women were expected to speak and exercise authority. Women were slave owners, and when they freed their slaves, they acted as patrons for those freedpeople. Women and men of lower social rank might appeal to a woman of higher status for assistance, including the use of her social influence in matters that concerned them. (See the discussion of property ownership and patronage in chapter 5.) In the presence of clients, the higher-status woman would be expected to speak (see also chapter 7). Such speech would not be deemed immodest because modesty looked different in differing circumstances, including the variations of social class.

The virtue of modesty also included sexual self-control. The virtuous woman was chaste, reserving sex only for her marriage. Although the standard was different, modesty as sexual self-control was a male virtue as well. Plutarch contrasted the *sōphrōn* husband with "men who have the intemperate, pleasure-loving natures of dogs or goats" (*Conj. praec.* 7). Having sex outside of marriage was not viewed as morally wrong for men, as it was for women. Nevertheless, sexual self-control for men promoted harmony within the marriage and was emblematic of self-discipline. Plutarch suggested that to avoid causing their wives pain and disturbance, husbands should not associate with other women (*Conj. praec.* 44).

In its ideal form, sexual modesty was not simply a matter of personal morality but promoted the stability of both the household and the city. This element of modesty may surprise modern readers, who tend to understand sexual morality as personal rather than political. But sōphrosunē was a virtue for political leaders. The first-century philosopher Musonius Rufus argued that good kings also exercised self-control (sōphrosunē). A wise king looked to the needs of the wider community and did not simply gratify his own desires. Musonius Rufus even saw the virtue embodied in the king's ability to control his tongue and dress appropriately (*Frag.* 8). Personal actions of dress and speech expressed the leader's concern for the well-being of the community. Thus, self-control was at the heart of what it meant to be a leader.

Latin thought also connected modesty to the good of the city. The Latin word *pudicitia* was not an exact equivalent of the Greek work sōphrosunē, although both can be translated as "modesty" in English. Pudicitia is more precisely translated as "sexual virtue."[4] However, like sōphrosunē, pudicitia connoted political or civic virtue, and not only personal morality. Pudicitia was not only a virtue but was also a divine being protecting the Roman emperor and people. In the early first century, Valerius Maximus wrote a book on the subject of pudicitia: "Whence should I invoke you, Chastity [Pudicitia], chief buttress of men and women alike? You dwell in the hearth consecrated to Vesta by ancient religion, you watch over the sacred couch of Capitoline Juno, you never leave your post on the pinnacle of the Palatine, the august habitation, and the most holy marriage bed of Julia" (6.1.1).[5] Pudicitia was a goddess inhabiting and watching over sacred Roman space, and in particular, the imperial household. Human pudicitia pleased the divine and contributed to the security of the city.

The story of Lucretia illustrates how modesty was understood as essential to a strong political order. Lucretia's tale narrated a key moment in the Republic's founding, when Rome turned from the tyranny of a king to democratic rule. The story presented the rejection of rule by kings as a defense of modesty. In a moment of drunken boasting, a group of husbands each wagered that his own wife had the greatest virtue. They secretly spied on the wives, and Lucretia won the contest. The daughters-in-law of the king sat at a lavish banquet, "but Lucretia, though it was late at night, was busily engaged upon her wool, while her maidens toiled about her in the lamplight as she sat in the hall of her house" (Livy, *Hist.* 1.57.9).[6] Enflamed by Lucretia's modesty, the king's son, Sextus Tarquinius, plotted to rape her. When she refused him, he threatened to dishonor her by killing her and leaving her dead body alongside that of a slave, creating the impression that Lucretia had committed adultery. Lucretia capitulated. She then called her male relatives, secured a promise of revenge, and killed herself. Her relatives drove Tarquinius into exile and founded the Republic to escape the tyranny of kings.

The repetition of Lucretia's story by the historians Livy (*Hist.* 1.57–59) and Valerius Maximus (6.1.1) suggested its importance in the beginning of the Roman empire. From their view, the defense of pudicitia motivated the establishment of the Roman Republic. Valerius wrote of Lucretia, "She killed herself with a sword she had brought concealed in her clothing and by so courageous a death gave the Roman people reason to change the authority of kings for that of Consuls" (6.1.1). The Romans bravely threw off rule by kings because it led to tyranny and was opposed to pudicitia.

On the one hand, Lucretia's story displayed the social inequalities of gender. The men around her had all the political and military authority. Tarquinius was a tyrant who took what he wanted without concern for others or for the city as a whole. In that context, Lucretia acted bravely to protect her honor and defend pudicitia. But she did so as one whose gender sharply limited her choices for action.

On the other hand, the story these writers told was one in which Lucretia acted heroically in dire circumstances to defend pudicitia and her community. She did not play the part of the helpless victim. Nor was her death required by her family or social stigma. Lucretia's suicide went against the wishes of her family. Her choices were limited by male power and cruelty, but she was not required to die. Instead, her suicide was told as a noble and brave act, one that protected her own honor and spurred the men in her family to similar acts of bravery for the sake of their people. Lucretia's story showed the importance of pudicitia to the stability of the political order.

The use of pudicitia to describe the emperor also pointed to the social and political importance of modesty. Pudicitia came to be closely associated with the imperial family. Valerius Maximus's words, quoted above, asserted that divine Pudicitia resided in the imperial household. Later, the goddess Pudicitia appeared on the reverse side of coins with the emperor Hadrian's image.[7] Augustus and other emperors drew on traditions like modesty and harmony within the family to cultivate an image of traditional virtue.

As I discussed in the last chapter, this emphasis on traditional virtues aided the transition from the more democratic government of the Republican era to the Imperial period during which the emperor consolidated political power in himself. In doing so, the emperor and his allies tapped into established social values. They characterized him as the father of the country, inviting the Roman people to view the emperor as a father, whose legal and moral power was well established within the family. Indeed, they claimed that the emperor displayed the domestic virtues of a good father. He was self-controlled and devoted to the gods, attributes that were already seen as important contributors to the well-being of the nation.

This social and political context helps to explain how some women were praised for modesty even as they pursued a political agenda. Modesty or self-control connected traditional household virtues with the capacity for leadership in the civic realm. The same judgment needed within the household also formed the foundation of a stable society.

To summarize: modesty was an ideal virtue for women in this period. But we should not imagine it as something that only placed limitations on a woman's ability to act. A robust notion of modesty helps to explain why modest women were also active contributors to their society. There were different expectations for men and women regarding modesty. Modesty for women entailed restraint in elaborate dress, and sexual self-control was required of women in a way that had no equivalent for men. Such differences displayed the gender inequalities that were part of the culture. However, modesty also indicated the capacity for good judgment, in both the family and the city. It was a virtue with political overtones related to the cohesion of the city.

INDUSTRY

Women in antiquity contributed in important ways to the well-being of their households. The production of food and clothing required considerable skill and labor, and the household was the center of that effort. Women worked in many of the stages of production (see chapter 6). As household managers, many oversaw the work of slaves and freedpeople. As I discussed in chapter 2, there was no separation of the "private" economy of the household and the "public" business interests of the family. Because of this overlap, women often worked in both the business of the family and in what modern readers might think of as more traditional "domestic" tasks.

Women in lower-class households labored to meet the basic needs of their families. Growing and cooking food, collecting water, and making clothing were both necessary and labor-intensive. In the cities, poorer classes often bought food and cloth, and in these cases women worked to produce the income necessary to acquire them. Slave women labored in all of these ways, and some undertook managerial or clerical tasks.

Elite women were less likely to engage in physical labor, but they still acquired knowledge and skills that contributed to the economic prosperity of the household. They supervised slaves and freedpeople who did the physical and managerial labor. They also established social ties that advanced the family's status and its interests. Maintaining social connections meant attending to the family's political and business relationships, which were important factors in the economic status of the household.

Thus, it is not surprising that one of the classic feminine virtues in antiquity was industry. The industrious woman promoted the well-being of her family in concrete ways. Whatever her social status or occupation, a woman's work contributed to the economic and social welfare of her family. The industrious woman would benefit her family through the economic value of her labor and through her pursuit of social status.

The iconic image of the industrious woman was the wool-worker. In the first century, women did not usually undertake all the steps in the long process required to produce clothing. Because cloth was available for purchase in the cities in this period, many women in urban areas would have purchased rather than produced cloth. Women in slaveholding families would have supervised the wool-work rather than performing it themselves. Men also participated in some parts of the process—as fullers or weavers, for example. Nevertheless, "wool-working" was shorthand for a woman's skill and productivity on behalf of her family, and it signified her virtue. In the story of Lucretia, recounted above, Lucretia's virtue became visible when the men saw her working wool late at night.

Wool-working signified women's virtue in many of the ancient sources, extending over a wide geographic area and many centuries. Burial inscriptions often praised women for their wool-working. The inscription honoring Amymone, also cited in chapter 1, was a classic example of wool-working as a symbol of feminine virtue: "Here lies Amymone, wife of Marcus, best and most beautiful, a worker in wool, pious, chaste, thrifty, faithful, a stayer at home" (*ILS* 8402). Amymone was praised with a long list of classical virtues, including *lanifica*, a "worker in wool." Along with the other virtues attributed to Amymone, *lanifica* suggested that Amymone fit the portrait of the ideal woman.

In another inscription, Murdia's son lauded her traditional feminine virtues: "My dearest mother deserved greater praise than all others, since in modesty, propriety, chastity, obedience, wool-working, industry, and loyalty she was on an equal level with other good women, nor did she take second place to any woman in virtue, work and wisdom in times of danger" (*CIL* 6.10230 [*ILS* 8394]).[8] Similarly, Turia's husband wrote about her in this way: "Why should I mention your personal virtues—your modesty, obedience, affability, and good nature, your tireless attention to wool-working, your performance of religious duties without superstitious fear, your artless elegance and simplicity of dress?" (*CIL* 6.1527, 31670 [*ILS* 8393]).[9] A funeral urn in the shape of a woman's wool basket (figure 3.2) conveyed a similar attribution of virtue in visual form.

The frequency of these examples suggests that wool-working was emblematic of feminine virtue. It characterized elite women like Turia and nonelite women like Amymone. Praising a woman for wool-working signified her virtue and thereby honored her, but it gives us little information about her daily activities. For example, as I mentioned in chapter 2, Suetonius portrayed the women of Augustus's family as making his clothing (*Aug.* 73). It is unlikely

FIGURE 3.2 Marble cinerary urn. Gift of Mrs. Frederick E. Guest, 1937
(37.129a, b) © The Metropolitan Museum of Art. Image source: Art
Resource, NY. Used by permission.

that Livia performed extensive labor in the production of her
family's clothing, although she may have overseen the production
process or contributed in a symbolic way. Suetonius's presentation
of her in this way reinforced the conventional virtue of the family as
a whole. Because of the honorific nature of the traditional virtues,
inscriptions that praised women for wool-working provide little information about these women's lives. Instead, they indicated a desire to present the woman being honored as a virtuous person.

Women's industry took many forms in addition to wool-
working. As I discuss in chapter 6, women had a number of
occupations in this period, although not as many as men had.
Burial inscriptions remembered slave women as attendants,
midwives, and clerics, among other things.[10] Many freedwomen
would have maintained their former occupations or, if they
married, joined in their husband's business. Papyri show women
contracting their own labor, managing farms, and apprenticing

slaves.[11] Women were wet nurses and elementary teachers.[12] As they pursued the economic interests of their families, any of these women might have been praised for industry or represented as "a worker in wool."

LOYALTY

Loyalty or devotion to one's family was highly prized in both women and men. Piety (or devotion; Latin, *pietas*; Greek, *eusebeia*) was due first and foremost to the gods, but familial piety was an extension of the same mindset. Children were expected to express loyalty to their parents, especially in caring for them during their old age, and spouses were to show similar loyalty to one another.

For women, sexual fidelity to one's husband was part of loyalty. In this sense, loyalty overlapped with modesty, which included sexual restraint. Married men could have sexual partners other than their wives. This behavior was not classified as adultery unless the other woman was married. Women, however, were expected to be chaste. A woman's sexual loyalty ensured that her children were her husband's progeny.

One expression of the value placed on marital loyalty was the praise of a woman as a *univira*, a woman married only once. Burial inscriptions and literary sources honored women for a single marriage.[13] But the value of the univira coexisted alongside cultural forces that encouraged women and men to remarry when widowed or divorced. Laws passed during the reign of Augustus gave financial incentives to people who remarried (see chapter 4). Yet even in this climate, women were also praised as *univirae*. The ideal represented the importance of fidelity to one's spouse and to their children.

Loyalty in marriage was not limited to sexual fidelity. It also included a broader sense of the couple's ability to consider their joint interests. Loyal spouses contributed to each other's well-being, even in difficult times. Because Roman law legally separated the financial affairs of a husband and wife (see chapter 4), the use of one's wealth to support the other, especially in a time of crisis, was one aspect of loyalty. Turia's husband highlighted the couple's mutual financial support. He cited his own willingness to fulfill a monetary obligation to Turia's family from his own resources. He also praised Turia for selling her jewelry to support him during a political crisis. The mutual support of the couple was recounted as evidence of their loyalty to one another.

Because the wife was viewed as the inferior partner in the marriage, her subordination of her interests to his often expressed the ideal of loyalty. Plutarch wrote, "When two notes are struck together, the melody belongs to the lower note. Similarly, every action performed in a good household is done by the agreement of the partners, but displays the leadership and decision of the husband" (*Conj. praec.* 11). The social expectations of loyalty were mutual but not equivalent.

Loyalty to family was not simply restrictive, for it also encouraged women's active pursuit of familial interests. Turia's husband praised her for wool-working and other traditional feminine virtues but also credited her for avenging the murder of her parents and for supporting young female relatives. Regarding her loyalty to him, he told this story:

> I was granted a pardon by Augustus, but his colleague Lepidus opposed the pardon. When you threw yourself on the ground at his feet, not only did he not raise you up, but in fact he grabbed you and dragged you along as if you were a slave. You were covered with bruises, but with unflinching determination you reminded him of Augustus Caesar's edict of pardon.... Although you suffered insults and cruel injuries, you revealed them publicly in order to expose him as the author of my calamities. (*CIL* 6.1527, 31670 [*ILS* 8393].[14]

Turia's loyalty in this case involved the pursuit of justice for her husband. Her active role did not diminish the traditional virtues that she was also said to exhibit. Indeed, her husband told the story as a shining example of her virtue.

Loyalty toward family and city was a virtue for both women and men. The virtue of *pietas* included loyalty to the state, gratitude to the gods, and devotion to family. In the familial category, pietas meant the reciprocal devotion of spouses, children and parents, and siblings.[15] But exemplary piety often involved political advocacy on behalf of one party. This was the case in Turia's advocacy for her husband. Similarly, Valerius Maximus praised Claudia, who intervened when a powerful enemy threatened her father (5.4.6). Valerius also lauded a son who demanded the removal of charges against his father (5.4.3). In these cases, men and women acted out familial devotion through bold political action.

Plutarch also recorded a number of stories praising the loyalty of women in his work, *On the Virtues of Women*. One was the story of Eryxo, whose husband was killed by a tyrant, Laarchus, who then sought Eryxo's hand in marriage. Eryxo tricked Laarchus to come into her chamber, where she had stationed her brother to kill him. Her actions expressed fidelity to her late husband but also served the community as a whole by removing the despot, Laarchus.

As the example of Eryxo suggests, loyalty as a virtue also meant devotion to one's people or city of origin. Eryxo's actions demonstrated faithfulness to her husband, but they also protected her city, Cyrene, from tyranny. Loyalty to the city was a quality that was praised in both men and women in this period. Inscriptions often proclaimed that the honoree was a "friend of the people" or devoted to the public good.

Other examples of civic loyalty included Junia Theodora, a first-century woman of Corinth honored in five inscriptions for her devotion to her people in neighboring Lycia (see chapter 5). She provided sanctuary for them during a time of political unrest and gave bequests to the nation. She was described as a friend and devoted patron of the Lycians and also as "living modestly."[16] The Lycians praised Junia Theodora for her devotion, expressed through political and financial support, and also for her traditional virtues.

Plutarch also praised the wife of Pythes, who interceded with her husband on behalf of the community. Pythes was a greedy and foolish ruler who consigned his people to work in the mines. His wife convinced him to release many of them for farming and other trades. Later, Pythes retired to an island, asking his wife to leave him in solitude but to send him dinner every day. "He passed the remainder of his life in this way, and his wife administered the government excellently, and gave the citizens relief from their miseries" (*Mulier. virt.* 27). This woman's loyalty to her husband and to her city went hand in hand. She took over the administration of the city on his behalf and was a better governor than he had been, but without neglecting her husband.

SUMMARY

The portrait of feminine virtue outlined above suggests a complex set of cultural norms and practices that shaped gender roles in the Roman world. Modesty, industry, and loyalty were embodied in multiple ways. Modesty encompassed a number of behaviors, including sexual fidelity, self-control, and wise use of household or communal resources. Similarly, industry referred both to labor within the household and to the pursuit of social connections and honor for the benefit of the family. Loyalty meant chastity for women but also financial generosity to family members or the use of social power in pursuit of familial actions.

Virtues like modesty, industry, and loyalty were complex and multivalent. The nuanced meanings of each virtue help to explain why active women were often praised or honored using domestic virtues. A woman who was an advocate for her community or family could still be called "modest." These cases often appear paradoxical to modern interpreters because we assume a narrow definition of modesty as subservience. But modesty's attribution to active women points to a more complex value.

The interaction between the virtues also created a social climate where being virtuous took on different forms. Instead of being confined to a single mold of feminine virtue, women pursued a variety of virtues under the particular circumstances their lives offered. This complexity also helps to explain why there is not simply a single role for women, defined by passivity and submission to men. The virtues supported a wider range of roles. The interaction of the virtues also suggests that active women were not countercultural renegades but were pursuing avenues that were socially acceptable.

The ability to see a wider set of possibilities for women's actions in antiquity is an important tool as we turn to the interpretation of evidence for women's economic and social roles and status. This complexity suggests interpreters may expect women's involvement in a host of activities that were social, economic, civic, and religious in nature. We should not dismiss evidence of women's participation in these arenas because we have previously decided these realms were off limits to women. Communities could perceive active women as virtuous and not see them as doing something forbidden to women. The social norms of the time supported action and leadership by women as well as submissive behavior.

The complexity of the virtues also creates the expectation that we may see tensions even within a single piece of evidence. For example, inscriptions often commended women for their service in civic offices or as benefactors while praising them using the familiar language of feminine virtues. The evidence suggests that the active roles women played did not conflict with traditional domestic virtues. As we turn to the New Testament, we may expect to see similar kinds of complexity in the roles and virtues of women.

SOCIAL NORMS AND VIRTUES
IN THE NEW TESTAMENT

Understanding the complexity in the ideals of female virtue in this period may change what interpreters see in the New Testament. Readers often assume that cultural norms of passivity and obedience to men restricted Christian women (and ancient women in general). A challenge in reading the New Testament, then, is to imagine that conventional virtues could be embodied in multiple ways, some of which encouraged women's leadership. The following examples are possibilities for reading the New Testament in light of this social context.

Modesty

The Greek word sōphrosunē (self-control or modesty) and its cognates appeared occasionally in the New Testament writings. In 1 Tim 2:8–15, for example, this word is found at the beginning and end of the instructions regarding women in worship (vv. 9, 15). In this context, it has often been translated "modesty" and, along with the instructions about silence (vv. 11–12), has conveyed to many modern readers the constraints placed upon women's behaviors by the demands of modesty.

In its historical context, however, sōphrosunē also conveyed the self-control required of Christian leaders. As a whole, 1 Tim 2:9–15 reflected conventional views. It upheld sōphrosunē in the wise use of household resources, as seen in the restraint shown through simple dress (vv. 9–10; see also 1 Peter 3:3). The control of the tongue in certain social situations was also evidence of self-control (vv. 11–12). In addition, the good character of one's family members (v. 15) reflected the leadership exercised by those in charge of the household.

Furthermore, in the same work, the author characterized leaders within this community by the same virtues. Bishops, for example, should be *sōphron* (1 Tim 3:2; NRSV, "sensible"). They were to be married once, and exercise self-control in their use of resources (e.g., "temperate," v. 2; "not a drunkard," v. 3) and their speech ("not quarrelsome," v. 3). They should manage their households well, evidence of which was seen in their children's behavior (v. 4). Likewise, male and female deacons were to be temperate (v. 11; cf. "not indulging in much wine," v. 8) and control their tongues ("not double-tongued," v. 8; "not slanderers," v. 11). Like bishops, they should manage their households well and be married only once (v. 12). Similar qualifications for the office of widow appeared in 1 Tim 5:9–10.

The complexity we have seen in the virtues suggests that the language of 1 Tim 2:8–15 made sense in its context in a different way than many modern readers have interpreted it. Modesty did not simply limit women's leadership but was also seen as the basis of good leadership. Women who were honored as modest could still exercise various forms of leadership in their households and communities. In the cultural context, we see similar statements of the "rules" of modesty, but we also see women enacting these rules in a variety of ways.

Even the advice that women should not teach or have authority over men (1 Tim 2:11–12) may be read in this context as a statement of agreed-upon virtues rather than a blanket prohibition of women's speech (see also chapter 7). The language of the passage fit within a cultural context where silence before those of higher social rank illustrated one's self-control. But some women in Christian communities were higher ranking than some of the men. For example, some women were deacons (1 Tim 3:11–13), and others were slave owners (1 Tim 6:1–2). The speech of such women would likely have been expected in certain contexts (see chapter 7). Women slave owners would have exerted authority over male slaves. Similarly, women deacons who spoke would not have been perceived as breaking the rules of modesty.

Industry

Glimpses of industrious women are also found in the New Testament. Luke portrayed Martha hard at work offering hospitality to a revered teacher (Luke 10:38–42). Martha's assumption that Mary should help her in this task may have been more than a petty dispute because it was likely that Martha understood her work as virtuous and therefore as something Jesus would encourage. Similarly, the efforts of the woman in the parable of the lost coin (Luke 15:8–10), sweeping and searching carefully, presented her as a virtuous laborer whose diligence was rewarded.

Tabitha (or Dorcas), the disciple of Acts 9:32–43 whom Peter raised from the dead, was likewise presented as an industrious woman. She was praised for her devotion "to good works and acts of charity" (9:36), which highlighted her labor and her actions as a patron to those in need. The widows gathered around her displayed the "tunics and other clothing that Dorcas had made while she was with them" (9:39). The community lifted up Dorcas's traditional virtues, including the production of clothing, which pointed to her industry and concern for others.

The designation of a woman as the good manager of her household also expressed industry. First Timothy elaborated with regard to the virtuous widow: "She must be well attested for her good works, as one who has brought up children, shown hospitality, washed the saints' feet, helped the afflicted, and devoted herself to doing good in every way" (1 Tim 5:10). The ideal woman the letter described was not passive but one who actively sought the good of those around her. Her virtue was seen in part through her management of the household (cf. 1 Tim 5:14; Titus 2:3–5).

The concern that widows might be lazy rather than industrious was the flip side of this conventional virtue. The author of 1 Timothy feared that young women who remained unmarried "learn to be idle, gadding about from house to house" (1 Tim 5:13). Because this concern represented common assumptions about marriage and industry, it seems unlikely that the actions of actual women in the community gave rise to this language.[17] Instead, the verse reflected a common view of marriage as a training ground for virtue because the wife was at the center of the production of food and clothing, management of slaves, raising children, and maintaining social connections. Such activities were expected to lead to the cultivated virtues of the "real widow" recognized by the community of 1 Timothy.

Loyalty

In the New Testament writings, the virtue of loyalty included devotion to God, city, and family. The overlap of these three is especially notable in 1 Timothy. The author repeatedly urged piety or devotion to God (*eusebeia*, e.g., 6:3, 11; and the related word, *theosebeia*, reverence for God, 2:10). The specific behaviors the letter extolled were meant to exhibit such piety. In particular, the author encouraged prayers "for kings and all who are in high positions, so that we may lead a quiet and peaceable life in all godliness (*eusebeia*) and dignity" (1 Tim 2:2; cf. Rom 13:1–7). This grouping of these topics made sense because devotion to God was similar to and overlapped with devotion to city and family.

First Timothy also expressed the importance of loyalty to one's family, and the writer connected this loyalty to religious devotion. The qualifications of Christian leaders listed in 1 Timothy included being married only once. Along with other virtues that represented the ideal of self-control, bishops (1 Tim 3:2; cf. Titus 1:6), deacons (1 Tim 3:12), and widows (1 Tim 5:9) were to be married only once. Loyalty to one's spouse was seen as evidence of self-control, an important capacity for leadership.

Other writings of the New Testament affirmed the value of loyalty to family members. The ideal of loyalty to one's spouse remained very consistent throughout the New Testament writings. In a variety of ways they express a preference for people to be married only once. One of these ways was through the prohibition of remarriage. In the Gospel of Mark, Jesus prohibited remarriage after divorce (Mark 10:10–12). Matthew's version of the saying allowed remarriage only for those who divorced because of the adultery of their spouse (Matt 19:9). Although modern interpreters tend to read these sayings only in relation to the practice of divorce, a primary concern of both passages was the question of remarriage following divorce. "Whoever divorces his wife and marries another commits adultery against her; and if she divorces her husband and marries another, she commits adultery" (Mark 10:11–12). Similarly, Paul preferred that widows remain unmarried if they could practice sexual self-control (1 Cor 7:8–9).

Other texts expressed the notion that familial obligations were reciprocal, though not equal. The expectation that honor was due to parents, for example, was found in instructions to children: "Children, obey your parents in the Lord, for this is right. 'Honor your father and mother'—this is the first commandment with a promise—'so that it may be well with you and you may live long on the earth'" (Eph 6:1–3; cf. Col 3:20). Parents were also instructed to treat children well (Eph 6:4; Col 3:21). In the Gospels, Jesus criticized the Pharisees for disregarding the commandment to honor father and mother in deference to oral tradition (Mark 7:9–13; Matt 15:3–6). These examples expressed the broader conception of familial loyalty as a virtue.

Jesus also acknowledged a tension among family members for those who placed allegiance to God (or Jesus) above loyalty to family. Jesus did not neglect the importance of familial loyalty, but he altered the terms: "Whoever does the will of God is my brother and sister and mother" (Mark 3:35). This kind of allegiance to the larger group was certainly also possible in the Greco-Roman world at large, where the emperor came to be known as the "father of the country." Allegiance to the community or the gods could, under certain circumstances, be put ahead of familial needs and still recognized as virtuous.

CONCLUSION

Many New Testament texts reflected the social hierarchy of this period. When other social factors were equal, men had greater status than women. Yet modern readers are inclined to see this language as more limiting for women than it may have been in practice. Early readers of New Testament texts recognized a variety of everyday expectations for women's behavior and were likely to have read these passages in ways that did not eliminate women's active leadership.

Christian women were encouraged to exhibit virtues that were widely acknowledged within the culture. The author of Titus expected the older women to teach the younger ones "to love their husbands, to love their children, to be self-controlled, chaste, good managers of the household, kind, being submissive to their husbands, so that the word of God may not be discredited" (Titus

2:4–5). Read against the background of the social norms of the first century, these words may not have suggested the picture of docility that modern readers expect. Readers of the letter to Titus may have understood these virtues in a more expansive way to include women like Turia, Junia Theodora, or the wife of Pythes. Like their Greco-Roman peers, the Christian women who displayed these virtues may also have been called upon to lead their communities in various ways.

Chapter 4

Marriage, Divorce,
and Widowhood

MODERN READERS OFTEN IMAGINE ANCIENT women's lives as being tightly circumscribed by the authority of their fathers or husbands. It is common to assume that men controlled women's lives and property—indeed, that women themselves were viewed and treated as property. Women passed from the authority of their fathers to that of their husbands. When widowed, they returned again to the authority of a male relative or a son; if they had no such relative, they were without resources and severely disadvantaged. This portrait may apply to women in many places or times, but it is inaccurate in many respects for the Roman world of the first and second centuries.

The legal status of women in the Imperial period differed in many ways from the common assumptions. This chapter addresses the legal status of women in marriage, divorce, and widowhood. Alterations in one's marital status often represented changes in social status as well, so the chapter also describes the social perceptions associated with marriage, divorce, and widowhood.

Although Roman law assumed women's inferiority to men, it also created legal pathways for women's independent status, property ownership, and participation in civic life. Along with the other social practices explored in this book, the legal material highlights the complex reality of women's status. On the one hand, the laws reflected the social expectation that women would pursue their economic and social interests. On the other, they never granted women official status equal to that of men.

One example of the law's assumption of women's inferiority is the Roman concept of *patria potestas* (paternal power). This legal term defined the authority of the father of the family (*pater familias*) over his children and slaves. *Potestas* meant that the father was formally the owner of the household property. Even when children became adults, they did not own property until their father died. Because legal texts defined potestas as a male capacity, classical historian Jane Gardner called potestas "the central asymmetry of Roman law."[1] Both male and female children were under their father's legal authority, but potestas was a legal right reserved only for males. Women were never described in law as having potestas.

Nevertheless, the capacities of women to assert themselves were also enshrined in Roman law. Roman men had potestas over their children and slaves but not over their wives. The impression that women passed from the authority of fathers to that of husbands came from an earlier period of Roman law, when another legal arrangement for marriage (known as marriage *cum manu*) was the norm. During the Imperial period, however, almost all marriages were *sine manu*, meaning that the woman did not transfer into the potestas of her husband. She remained part of her father's family and thus was under his authority until he died. Both sons and daughters were under the potestas of their fathers during his lifetime. When he died, they became legally independent or *sui iuris*. At that point, they could own property, and a son became the *pater familias* of his own household. Both law and custom assumed that sons and daughters inherited their father's property in equal portions.

Furthermore, the legal rights of the "father of the family" or pater familias often applied to women, even though the terminology suggested that the pater familias was male. Classicist Richard Saller has argued that legal texts commonly used pater familias to denote an estate owner rather than the male head of household.[2] Indeed, a son whose father had died became the pater familias with respect to his property even if he was not a father of children. Similarly, the term pater familias described the legal rights of the property owner in a way that was not limited to men. Many women owned property and exercised the legal rights of the pater familias. Thus, women were "fathers of the family" with respect to their own property. (For more on women's property ownership, see chapter 5.) Although the law excluded women from potestas, the broader rights of the pater familas applied to women as well as men.

Like potestas, practices of legal guardianship also sent mixed signals about the status of women. A woman who was sui iuris (that is, one whose father had died) needed the signature of a guardian (or tutor) to legalize certain kinds of transactions. Specifically, the guardian consented to the sale of property classified in law as *res mancipi*: slaves, certain kinds of livestock, and land in Italy. Originally, the guardianship of women gave oversight of these types of property to a family member designated by the woman's father. The jurist Gaius, writing in the second century, described the initial rationale for the practice: "For the ancients wanted women, even if they are of full age, to be in guardianship (*tutela*) on account of their lightmindedness" (*Inst.* 1.144).[3] The law assumed that women could not be trusted to secure the best interests of the family and therefore their property had to be monitored.

By the first century, however, guardians exercised little if any control over women's property. Women often chose their own guardians. They could even choose their own freed slaves, men who were obliged to honor the wishes of their former master. Gaius acknowledged the perceived reason for the law, as noted above, but wrote that the rationale no longer made sense:

> Almost no reason of value appears to recommend that women of full age be in *tutela*. For the reason which is commonly believed, that since they are very often deceived due to their lightmindedness, it was right for them to be ruled by the authority of tutors, seems to be specious rather than true. Indeed,

women who are of full age transact business deals for themselves, and in certain cases the tutor interposes his authority for the sake of legal form; often he is even forced by the praetor to give his authority against his will. (*Inst.* 1.190)[4]

In Gaius's day, guardianship was still in place but had been emptied of its power. Many women undertook desired economic transactions without the interference of a guardian.

The legal status of women was thus something of a mixed bag. The law formally acknowledged male superiority and granted potestas to men alone. Many women in the Imperial period were in the potestas of their fathers or had a guardian. Yet this formal validation of male control obscured the reality that women owned property and that their guardians had little influence over their affairs. Although the father's authority was substantial, it applied to sons as well as to daughters and therefore should not be seen as restrictive for women only. The legal status of women contributed to the social practices that made possible women's leadership and civic participation.

MARRIAGE

As noted above, marriage in this period was largely sine manu, meaning that a Roman woman remained in the legal authority (potestas) of her father and became legally independent (sui iuris) at his death. She was never in the potestas of her husband. This capacity of women to own and control property was a basis for power within the marital relationship and within the community, for wealth brought social influence that could benefit both family and city.

Consent to Marry

A marriage was formed by the consent of the two spouses. Although a ritual or celebration often marked the beginning of a union, marriage did not require a government official or legal documentation. In the eyes of the law, marriage began at the time the couple consented and considered themselves to be married. A legal agreement often specified the property included in the dowry, but no marriage license or registration signaled the change in status to a married person.

For a couple who were not legally independent (sui iuris), the consent of the father was also required. A father's potestas gave him the legal authority to select a spouse for his child. The opinion of the third-century jurist, Paulus, likely reflected the earlier period as well: "Marriage is not able to occur unless all consent, that is, those who join together and those in whose power they are" (*Dig.* 23.3.3).[5] The requirement of consent by all parties created an interesting tension. On the one hand, the father's authority meant he could marry his daughter to whomever he chose. On the other hand, the woman's consent was necessary for the marriage to be valid.

The father's authority over his daughter was an important principle, but its practical effects on women should not be overstated. For example, although the law did not mention the mother's consent to her child's marriage, in practice mothers played significant roles in betrothing their daughters and sons.[6] Furthermore, about half of women were legally independent at their first marriage because their fathers had already died.[7] Men tended to be older than women at the time of marriage—a woman often married in her late teens and a man in his mid- to late twenties. Because of this, men were older when they became parents. By the time a daughter was of an age when she would marry, it was possible that her father had already died. The absence of a father did not mean a daughter was free to do as she pleased. She was likely to consider the wishes of her family, even though she was not legally obligated in the same way.

Marriages often expressed familial status and interests. Both men and women sought marriages that improved the interests of their families. Roman culture did not idolize romantic love or a young person's rebellion. Instead, different cultural forces shaped people's desires. In some ways, marriage enacted the obligation to one's family of origin, whose choice of a spouse reflected the family's interests. But marriage also forged new loyalties to the family created by the marriage and to one's in-laws. Ideally, both sides benefited by linking their interests together.

The cultural ideal of marriage was not simply dutiful but also affectionate. The expectation was that a couple would join together and share mutual interests, but they would also be bound through affection to one another. Musonius Rufus wrote of marriage as a place where the husband and wife lived together in harmony and cared for one another (*Frag.* 13a). Many burial inscriptions underscored this social value, citing the harmonious nature of the marriage as evidence of the virtue of the deceased.[8] Although the inscriptions do not tell us what the marriage was like in practice, they do reveal that spouses idealized their marriages as harmonious.

Dowry

Women were commonly married with a dowry, which was a portion of the property they would inherit from their fathers. The husband received the dowry to use for the duration of the marriage. Thus, the husband had legal authority over a portion of the wife's property.

However, society viewed the dowry as the woman's property, and it had to be returned to her in the event of divorce or the death of her husband. The husband could not sell the dowry, but he could benefit from its use or investment during the course of the marriage. Moreover, women often had ownership and control of property that was not part of their dowry and therefore not under the husband's control.

The dowry practices of Roman law reinforced the notion that men had greater power than women. However, that power was not without limits. The dowry represented the relative power of a husband over his wife, for he controlled a portion of her property during marriage. However, in this period the dowry did not convey a more extreme imbalance of power, such as one might find in a situation where the husband controlled all of the woman's property or retained the dowry in his possession forever.

Some evidence suggests that the dowry gave women influence over their husbands. For example, the late first-century poet Martial wrote, "You all ask why I don't want to marry a rich wife? I don't want to be my wife's wife. The matron . . . should be below her husband. That's the only way man and woman can be equal" (*Epigrams* 8.12).[9] Martial's verse conveyed the expectation that wives should be subordinate to husbands. He also suggested that a woman's wealth increased her status, so that a wealthy wife could have higher status than her husband. Although Martial viewed this scenario negatively, his comment also indicated the reality that a woman's wealth contributed to her social status, which could be higher than her husband's. Women whose dowry made a substantial contribution to their husband's wealth may have had influence over their husbands.

Social Status in Marriage

Women gained status through marriage and childbearing. In the Greek conception, a young female was a girl (*parthenos* or *korē*) until she married, at which time she became a woman or wife, *gunē*. Similarly, the Latin *matrona* signified the role wives took on as overseers of the household. A girl who left her parents' household to marry changed status and became a woman. Suzanne Dixon wrote, "A Roman matron, whether legally in the power of her husband or father or *in tutela*, had a certain status of respectability as mistress of the household which was enhanced if she became a mother and further elevated if she became a widowed mother."[10] A good marriage alliance brought social connections that benefited the woman and her family. It also signaled adulthood and a change of status within the community.

Roman law also codified this change in status at marriage. The emperor Augustus passed laws that encouraged marriage and the production of citizens. Known as the *Lex Julia et Poppaea* of 18 B.C.E. and 9 C.E., these laws communicated the importance of marriage for all citizens, male and female. Only married people could receive a large legacy from someone who was not a close relative. Married men had priority in receiving certain official appointments. Widowed people had to remarry within two or three years to retain the legal benefits of a married person. These rules targeted the elite, who were the only persons likely to inherit a large legacy from someone to whom they were not closely related or to serve in higher levels of the Roman bureaucracy. But even as the rules targeted the wealthy, they sent a message about the importance of marriage and elevated the status of married people more broadly.

Similarly, the *ius liberorum* gave incentives to men and women to bear and raise children. This legal status was conferred on freeborn men and women who had three children, or on freed people with four children. The right released women from the requirement of a guardian and men from the burden of serving as a guardian. Spouses with children could bequeath a greater proportion of their property to the other spouse.[11] Children brought legal benefits and added social status.

Through the marriage legislation, the emperor acknowledged and reinforced the civic importance of marriage and childbearing. Society viewed marriage, not as a personal or private matter, but one that had bearing on the stability of the wider community. Faithful and harmonious marriages were a civic good, the bedrock upon which other communal relations rested. Thus, as Kristina Milnor argued, the ius liberorum was "more a recognition of civic responsibility than a reflection of actual reproduction."[12] This rationale helps to explain why the emperor would grant the right to those without the requisite number of children—as, for example, in the case of Pliny the Younger (*Ep.* 10.2; cf. 10.94–95). The ius liberorum brought honor to its recipients, and was cited in inscriptions as a way of conveying the status of the one being praised. Even after guardianship was no longer a legal requirement, women still cited the achievement of the right, presumably because of the honor it carried.[13]

The connection between domestic virtue and civic responsibility found in the ius liberorum was consistent with the social and political changes of the first and second centuries. As

I discussed in chapters 2 and 3, the emperor reinforced the civic nature of traditional domestic virtues. Augustus emphasized his own role as "father of the country" and the domestic virtues of his family. He sought to encourage civic participation by emphasizing the importance of long-held domestic virtues. The pursuit of these virtues brought honor and influence to the women and men who achieved them.

Marital Harmony

Social norms idealized the husband as the dominant partner within marriage. Men had higher social status than women when other factors were equal. Two partners with roughly equal wealth and family influence were viewed as a good match for marriage. The husband therefore had higher status due to his gender. In addition, husbands were customarily five to ten years older than their wives. This age difference also gave the husband greater status.

As seen in the quote from Martial, cited above, wealthy wives were viewed negatively because their wealth upset this balance of power, leaving the husband in the position of lower status. Plutarch also noted the importance of this balance and the disruptive potential of a wealthy wife: "There is no profit in a rich wife, unless she makes her life and character resemble and harmonize with her husband's" (*Conj. praec.* 14). This short quotation displays a number of important aspects of the social understanding of marriage. Plutarch expressed the idea that the wife had lower status than the husband, but also that she had social standing and influence. Furthermore, he pointed to the ideal of harmony in marriage, a goal that could be compromised by a powerful wife.

Literary sources frequently expressed the ideal of marital harmony. The Roman historian Tacitus praised the union between Domitia Decidiana and Agricola: "Their life was singularly harmonious, thanks to mutual affection and putting each other first" (*Agr.* 6).[14] Written works like this one presented the merits of the subject in an idealized form; therefore, they cannot give modern readers a clear picture of the relationship between the two parties. However, they drew on qualities that were meant to be recognized by readers as ideal, thus suggesting that standards like harmony were widely embraced.[15]

Plutarch elaborated on this goal in *Advice to the Bride and Groom*: "When two notes are struck together, the melody belongs to the lower note. Similarly, every action performed in a good household is done by the agreement of the partners, but displays the leadership and decision of the husband" (*Conj. praec.* 11). Plutarch went on to point out activities that were likely to irritate both husbands and wives, which each should avoid. Men were to dine with their wives and share conversation with them (*Conj. praec.* 15). Wives were not to seek the company of gossiping women who sowed discord (*Conj. praec.* 40). Both husbands and wives should seek not to offend one another (*Conj. praec.* 39). The advice did not assume husbands and wives to be equal, but it conveyed the notion that both parties contributed to and influenced the other in their relationship.

The ideal of harmony within marriage assumed the priority of men, yet it also acknowledged that the marital relationship was not one of simple dominance. Plutarch noted: "The husband should rule the wife, not as a master rules a slave, but as the soul rules the body, sharing her feelings and growing together with her in affection. That is the just way" (*Conj. praec.* 33). The marital relationship was not domineering, as the master-slave relationship was; instead, it was meant to produce pleasure for both partners. It was a relationship of harmony, like that of the soul and body. The male was clearly envisioned as the superior party, but at the same time both spouses were required to act with deference toward the other.

The importance of harmony in this period may reflect the economic and social influence of women. A woman's property benefited her husband, not because he controlled it, but because she could use her property to contribute to the family's honor. The ideal of harmony suggested that the couple came to view their interests as shared. Plutarch wrote, "Scientists tell us that liquids mix completely: so should the bodies, resources, friends, and connections of a married couple" (*Conj. praec.* 34). In reality

Roman law insisted that marital assets not be mixed. Wives and husbands had separate property, and in this period many women attained substantial wealth.

A successful marriage achieved Plutarch's ideal not when spouses combined their resources but when they understood their social and political interests as intertwined.[16] An example from an earlier period is the funeral oration about Turia, cited in chapter 3. (A fragment of the inscription is depicted in figure 4.1.) Turia's husband described property as if it were jointly held: "We divided our duties in such a way that I had the guardianship of

FIGURE 4.1 Funerary inscription known as Laudatio Turiae. © Ministero dei beni e delle attività culturali e del turismo—Soprintendenza Speciale per I Beni Archeologici di Roma. Used by permission.

your property and you had the care of mine." Yet the rest of the oration clarifies that both parties retained control of their property and used it for the sake of the other. Turia promised dowries to female relatives to secure honorable marriages. But her husband and sister's husband fulfilled the obligations from their own resources. Turia's husband went on to praise her for providing for his needs from her own riches during his exile. The examples suggested an ideal marriage because the couple understood their needs as intertwined.

Women in the Provinces

In the provinces, local laws and customs governed much of the daily life of those who were not Roman citizens. It is difficult to know what kinds of legal arrangements existed in many parts of the territory Rome controlled. Local customs may have prevailed that were very different from those of Roman law because Rome did not force its legal standards on noncitizens. However, there is also evidence that local populations adopted Roman social practices through assimilation—not because they were forced to, but as a way of adapting to the changing social norms. It seems most likely, however, that a mixture of Roman and local practices existed. To complicate matters, the adoption of Roman practices likely varied from place to place. To explore the matter, we must look at the evidence available in different areas. Some inscriptions and papyri show evidence of marriage and dowry practices in the provinces. Other evidence points to patterns of women's control and ownership of property. There are a few significant differences between Roman and local practices, but there are also important ways in which they overlap.

For example, papyri from the Judean desert show a mixture of legal practices, some of which are distinctively Jewish while others resemble Greek and Roman legal documents. The Babatha archive is a collection of papyrus documents held by a woman named Babatha in the early second century.[17] Babatha was married to a man named Jesus, and they had a son, also named Jesus. After her husband died, Babatha entered into a polygamous marriage with

Judah, a man who may have been married to another woman, Miriam, with whom he had a daughter, Shelamzion.[18] Since Roman law forbade polygamy, Babatha's documents reflected local customs. Her marriage to Judah would not be acknowledged under the law if they were Roman citizens. However, the document does not confirm that polygamy was widespread among Jews. There is some other evidence for polygamy in this period, though many Jewish sources also attest marriage to one spouse.[19] Although the papyri suggest that some Jewish people were polygamous, the sources also confirm a variety of acceptable practices.

In other cases, where modern readers might expect distinctive Jewish practices to appear, we find similarities to Greek and Roman practices. For example, the Hebrew Bible described Jewish dowry practices that expect a bride price rather than a dowry (Hebrew, *mohar*). This was an amount paid by the husband to the wife's father (e.g., Gen 34:12; Exod 22:17). After the New Testament period, rabbinic sources specified a *ketubba*, an arrangement that provided a payment from husband to wife if the couple divorced. Both the mohar and the ketubba were distinctively Jewish marital arrangements. However, neither one is widely attested in this period. The Greek version of the Hebrew Bible known as the Septuagint (LXX) translates the Hebrew word *mohar* as dowry (Greek, *phernē*), which suggests that the dowry was understood as the normative practice. The ketubba is occasionally attested in the papyri, but not as commonly as the dowry. Furthermore, some Jewish dowry agreements were written in Greek, which again expresses similarity to the wider culture in conventions regarding marriage. There does not seem to be a single Jewish form of marriage. Some marriages were similar in their legal structure to Greek and Roman practices.[20]

Women in Egypt also married with dowry agreements, some of which have been discovered among papyrus documents.[21] As in Roman society, dowries returned to the woman in the case of divorce, and a woman usually owned property that was not part of the dowry, including land or slaves inherited from her parents. One distinctive marriage practice among Egyptians was the marriage of siblings. This was formally prohibited for Roman citizens but was possible among Egyptians. It is difficult to tell to what extent sibling marriage occurred in this period. But even among siblings, women were married with dowries that would be returned in the case of divorce.[22]

In Asia Minor there is little direct evidence for local marriage and dowry customs. However, there is a good deal of evidence that married and unmarried women owned property and exerted influence as patrons (see chapter 5). The similarities in the property ownership and activities of women suggest that marriage practices may have been similar as well. Women may have married with a dowry that was returned to them in the case of divorce or the death of their husbands. Women also owned property that was not included in their dowries, which they used to make the benefactions that are honored in inscriptions.

One difference in Greek-speaking areas was that the woman's husband was usually her guardian during marriage. This role gave the husband influence over the woman's use of her property because certain kinds of transactions required his signature. Even when women had legal ownership of property, we should not assume that their decision making was independent of familial concerns. The honor and status of the family was always factored into decisions about civic donations, and it is likely that family members influenced each other's use of property.[23]

Slaves and Marriage

Roman law did not recognize relationships between slaves as marriages. The laws on marriage largely existed to clarify property relations between citizen spouses and their children. Enslaved spouses were owned by their masters, and their children were also born as slaves. Property they held reverted back to their master upon death. Slave marriages were not illegal, but they fell into a different category in Roman law.[24]

Not surprisingly, however, many slaves considered their own relationships to be marriages. Although the law did not acknowledge them as husband and wife, some slaves dedicated burial inscriptions with these terms. Latin inscriptions often used the specific legal term for an enslaved spouse (*contubernalis* e.g., *CIL* 6.16832). However, some used the same vocabulary and terms of affection as free couples. For example, Victorinus dedicated an inscription to Nonia Hieronis, his well-deserving and most dutiful wife (*coniunx, CIL* 6.23044).[25] Similarly, Greek inscriptions often refer to the slave couple simply as husband and wife. For example, one inscription stated in conventional terms who was buried in a tomb: "Pheidias, Maron, Eudaimon, slaves of Archepolis, constructed the tomb for themselves and father and mother and for the wife of Pheidias, Elpis, and the wife of Maron, Soteria, and for the children of the aforerecorded wives of Pheidias and Maron, but for no other is it permitted [to be buried]" (*TAM* 2.1032; cf. *TAM* 2.1020).[26] The record of slaves naming their wives contradicts what we might expect from reading only the legal texts and is a reminder that slaves' lives were not well represented by the writings of their masters. Many relationships fell outside of Roman law but were considered to be marriages by those who participated in them.

Similarly, marital laws did not include relationships between a master and slave. Masters could exploit their slaves sexually if they chose but could not legally marry them. Male slave owners were allowed to free their female slaves and then marry them.[27] This legal practice reinforced the social distinction between slave and free, for Roman citizens could not be slaves, and the law recognized only citizen marriages. (For more on social status and slavery, see chapter 5.)

The legal situation was different for female masters, who were not allowed to marry their freed slaves. This distinction reflected the anxiety that wives would have sex with male slaves in the household. Although many women disliked their husbands' sexual use of slave women, the culture viewed these relationships as his prerogative and supported them by law. The legal requirement also reinforced the social expectation that husbands should have higher status than wives.

DIVORCE

Like marriage, divorce required no legal documentation or court procedures under Roman law. A couple who no longer consented to be married was divorced in the eyes of the law. Either the husband or the wife could initiate a divorce.

Legal transactions might accompany a divorce if the return of the dowry was disputed. As noted above, society viewed the dowry as the woman's property, and it had to be returned to her in the event of a divorce. An exception to this was that an adulterous wife could forfeit a portion of her dowry. Women could sue in court if the dowry was not returned to them for some reason.

One such legal document records a dispute over the return of a woman's dowry. Tryphaine asserted that she was married with a down payment on her dowry of clothing worth forty drachmas and twenty drachmas in silver coins. She asked the authorities to intervene to ensure the repayment of the dowry (*BGU* 4.1105). Tryphaine's divorce became visible to modern readers because her husband did not return her dowry. In many cases, a divorce may have proceeded according to custom without a need for legal action. Because of this, it is difficult to tell how common divorce was among the general population.

The Roman elite sometimes divorced in order to establish political and social alliances with another family. For example, Livia and Augustus's marriage lasted fifty-two years, but it came about after his divorce of Scribonia and hers of Tiberius Claudius Nero. Augustus had also been married to Clodia Pulchra, whom he divorced to marry Scribonia. Classicist Susan Treggiari estimated that one in six elite marriages ended in divorce.[28] Romans certainly also valued long and harmonious marriages. Yet the ideal of the faithful, single marriage was sometimes in tension with the political value of marriage for the families involved. In some cases, it was deemed worthwhile to break off a marriage for the sake of a more fruitful social connection.[29]

Augustus's marriage laws required divorce in the case of adultery by the wife. A husband who retained an adulterous spouse could be charged as a pimp.[30] Some Jewish sources also encouraged divorce in the case of adultery (e.g., Sir 25:29; 'Erub. 41b).

Jewish women also initiated divorces in this period. Many interpreters have assumed they did not because the biblical texts and later rabbinic writings indicated only that husbands could give their wives a certificate of divorce (Deut 24:1; m. Giṭ. 9:10). Yet sources from the New Testament period suggest that some Jewish women initiated divorce in ways similar to their Roman counterparts. Although he disapproved of the practice, the first-century Jewish philosopher Philo of Alexandria wrote about women divorcing their husbands "for any cause" (*Spec.* 3.30). The historian Josephus mentioned two elite Jewish women, Drusilla and Mariamne, who divorced their husbands in order to marry other men (*Ant.* 20.143, 147). Indicating that divorce occurred also among nonelite women, one papyrus from the Judean desert likely recorded a writ of divorce from a wife to her husband (*P. Seʾelim* 13).[31] Although it is impossible to know how widespread this practice was, the evidence available suggests that it was possible for Roman, Greek, and Jewish women to divorce their husbands.

WIDOWHOOD

Because husbands were typically older than wives, many women became widows. Citing data from Egypt, Richard Saller estimated that half of women were not married by the time they reached their late thirties.[32] Since almost everyone married in this period, these statistics show that many women experienced the death of their husbands and became widows.

Augustus's marriage laws required widows and widowers to remarry within two or three years to maintain the legal benefits of marriage. This requirement created the impression for some interpreters that everyone was forced to marry, and to remarry when widowed or divorced. Yet it is important to clarify that it was not illegal to be unmarried. The laws gave financial benefits to married people, and especially to elite Romans. This distinction helps to explain the evidence that many women did not remarry.[33] Younger and wealthier women were more likely to remarry, while older or lower-class women were unlikely to remarry. Although Augustus's laws valorized marriage as evidence of responsible citizenship, other factors affected the decision to remarry.

Society assigned a range of meanings to widowhood. As I noted in chapter 3, praise of the *univira*—a woman married only once—expressed the ideal of loyalty to one's husband. Some widows were described as virtuous, in part because people interpreted their remaining unmarried as loyalty to their husbands.

Widows could also be criticized as immodest or lazy. In his defense of Caelius, Cicero drew on cultural assumptions regarding the danger of a widow who lived without restraint: "a frisky widow living frivolously, a rich widow living extravagantly, an amorous widow living a loose life" (*Cael.* 38).[34] Similarly, Petronius's character Eumolpus told stories of "the fickleness of women," including that of the widow of Ephesus (*Satyricon* 110–112). Although supposedly very chaste and loyal to her husband, she quickly turned away from him after his death. Not only did she have sex with a soldier but she also desecrated her husband's body in order to aid the soldier. Such stories conveyed the fear that widows might turn from their fidelity. It is difficult to verify whether either Cicero's criticism of the widow or Petronius's story described the actions of actual women. But they displayed anxiety about widows and warned of potential difficulties.

The meaning and experience of widowhood depended on one's social status and wealth. Because women owned and inherited property, not all widows were poor. A majority of Roman women were legally independent (sui iuris) by the time they became widows. They already owned and managed their property. When the husband died, a widow inherited a portion of her husband's estate. If the couple had children, she inherited a greater portion of his property. Her dowry also returned to her upon his death. Thus, many widows continued to have financial resources at their disposal. Such widows were not necessarily free from the constraint of familial expectations of married women.

They still were likely to pursue the interests of their children and other family members. Yet they had some resources at their disposal and may have controlled more property than before their husbands died.

Some widows were very wealthy people of high status. The empress Livia, for example, became a widow when Augustus died in 14 C.E. She lived another fifteen years and remained an extremely influential person. Among examples of the local elite of Egypt, Petronia Magna dedicated a shrine to Aphrodite (*OGIS* 2.675). The inscription mentioned her children, but no husband, suggesting that she was likely a widow. Although such evidence exists for elite widows, wealthy women who were young were likely to remarry. These women and the men they married gained further prestige through the marriage and the shared financial resources it brought.

Some Jewish people had similar practices of inheritance by wives. In the apocryphal books of the Bible, Judith was one example of a wealthy widow. "Her husband Manasseh had left her gold and silver, men and women slaves, livestock, and fields; and she maintained the estate" (Jud 8:7). Judith was a fictional example of the kind of social and religious influence a wealthy widow might have. She was viewed as pious and wise, and when she called the elders of the town, they came and listened to her (Jud 8:9–11). The story assumed that its readers were familiar with such practices and would not find them surprising.

Women of more modest means also inherited property from their husbands, albeit in lesser amounts. As I discuss in chapter 5, many women owned and managed farmland and ran businesses. Business and legal records did not always record women's marital status because there was not any need to mention it. One cannot tell if a woman with independent business interests was a wife who owned her own business or a widow who inherited one from her husband. The large number of widows in society suggests that either one was possible.

Many widows were certainly worse off financially than when they were married. Women whose families were poor were likely to remain poor as widows. If a woman's husband were a wage laborer, she would not have an easy way to replace the income he earned. Some people targeted widows as prey to steal from them or take their businesses. Yet we should not expect that all widows experienced a marked drop in economic circumstances and became poor.

Financial care for elderly parents was both a moral and legal obligation across the varied subcultures of the Mediterranean. The Old Testament commandment to honor parents (Exod 20:12; Deut 5:16) was a well-known Jewish example. Philo of Alexandria elaborated on this teaching in the first century: "For children have nothing of their own which does not come from their parents. . . . Piety (Greek: *eusebeia*) and religion are the queens among the virtues" (*Decal.* 118). Greek and Roman writings expressed similar norms. Just as parents were obliged to care for children, children should care for parents in their old age.[35] By the second century, Roman law also reflected the expectation that children should support elderly parents (*Cod. Just.* 5.25).

Many children cared for their widowed mother by bringing her into their homes. One letter from a woman to her brother exhorted him to treat their mother well.[36] However, the impression that all widows fell under the male authority of sons requires revision. Mothers retained their social standing and authority when they became widows.[37] No legal or social conventions subjected a mother to her son's authority. Furthermore, census records in Egypt show that many women lived in households of women with no male adult present.[38] There was certainly no legal requirement that male family members supervise widows. A variety of arrangements were possible, and widows probably made such decisions based on their financial situation and family composition.

SUMMARY

Marriage added to a person's social status. It signified adulthood and full participation in society. The social norms of the period identified marriage as something that benefited the social order. Marriage forged alliances with another family, which brought social connections and financial resources. Generally speaking, marriage meant an increase in status to men and women.

Both inside and outside of marriage, men had greater social status and more legal rights than their female peers. Social pressures suggested wives were expected to subordinate their interests to their husbands to a greater extent than husbands accommodated their wives. Although the requirements of loyalty were reciprocal, they were never equal.

Nevertheless, a number of legal factors gave women standing within marriage. Women owned property that was not controlled by their husbands. Their dowries returned to them in the case of divorce or death. They could initiate a divorce. Structurally, these features gave women significant power within their marital relationships.

There was a great deal of variety in the circumstances of women's lives. A woman's wealth or her status as slave or free, for example, likely affected her circumstances more than whether she was married or widowed.[39] A wealthy woman had status and social influence regardless of her marital status. Poorer women had lower status and would be more likely to suffer financially from a death or divorce. Some marriage practices seem to have varied according to local practices, although there is widespread evidence for women's ownership of property and ability to initiate a divorce.

MARRIAGE, DIVORCE, AND WIDOWHOOD IN THE NEW TESTAMENT

Interpreters of the New Testament have often imagined that women were strictly controlled within marriage and left powerless when widowed or divorced. However, the above discussion suggests that women had greater capacity for independent action than we have often assumed. Although the capacities of women varied a great deal, a woman's agency was affected by her social standing or legal independence more than by her marital status. As we read the New Testament, we should not presume that practices of marriage, divorce, and widowhood had uniform effects on women.

Marriage

In the New Testament, Eph 5:22–33 stated the ideal of harmony within marriage. Although husband and wife were to work together in harmony, the relationship was never thought to be egalitarian. The letter positioned the male as the figurehead and leader of the family. Women were expected to defer to their husbands, as to others of higher social rank. First Peter 3:1–7 conveyed similar expectations, presenting a wife's deference as a virtue.

In approaching a text like Ephesians or 1 Peter, however, modern readers should remember that these ideals of harmony and deference in marriage existed alongside expectations that women take on active roles. Wives were managers and made decisions about household resources (see chapter 6). They pursued the interests of their families. As in the example of Turia, above, the devoted wife might have implemented a political agenda out of loyalty to her parents or husband. Turia fulfilled the cultural ideal of the obedient wife, but she was hardly a passive person. She had property under her control and supported relatives, including her husband. As I discuss in chapter 5, Turia also pursued the political interests of her husband against a powerful male opponent. Her actions as a virtuous spouse differ from the assumptions of many modern interpreters, who suggest that Eph 5:22–33 reflected cultural norms that sharply restricted women's actions. In the world of the New Testament, women were characterized with traditional feminine virtues even as they actively pursued the interests of their families.

Some examples from the New Testament show the coexistence of both the restrictive norms and the active leadership of women. Colossians had language similar to that of Ephesians about wives being subject to husbands (Col 3:18–19), but at the end Paul also greeted "Nympha and the church in her house" (Col 4:15). To readers of the time, Nympha's leadership would not have seemed to contradict the earlier statements about women's roles. Virtuous wives and widows actively pursued social, familial, and political goals, and in doing so they did not reject cultural norms. The acknowledgment of women leaders existed alongside the marital ideals.

Another example of a virtuous and active married woman in the New Testament was Prisca (or Priscilla). Although mentioned with her husband, Aquila, the plural verbs that applied to the couple pointed to Prisca's active involvement. Writing to the church in Corinth, Paul sent greetings from Aquila and Prisca, together with the church in their house (1 Cor 16:19). Later, when the couple had returned to Rome, Paul greeted "Prisca and Aquila, who work with me in Christ Jesus, and who risked their necks for my life" (Rom 16:3–4). The author of Acts also mentioned Priscilla and Aquila as tentmakers who worked with Paul in this trade. Acts recorded their joint efforts to correct the teachings of Apollos (Acts 18:1–3, 26). In every instance the couple were mentioned together and described as acting in the same way. Paul characterized Prisca's behavior as both active and exemplary.

Paul's suggestion that people might not marry at all (1 Cor 7) is unusual in this cultural context. Paul stated that it was preferable for the unmarried to remain so, though he conceded that marriage was necessary for some. "To the unmarried and the widows I say that it is well for them to remain unmarried as I am. But if they are not practicing self-control, they should marry" (1 Cor 7:8–9). His views reflected a culture in which marriage was by far the norm; even Paul seems to have expected it would remain this way for many Christians.

Divorce

Many readers of the New Testament are familiar with Jesus's prohibitions of divorce. Responding to the Pharisees' question,

"Is it lawful for a man to divorce his wife?" (Mark 10:2), Jesus presented divorce as a concession to human "hardness of heart" (10:5). He concluded by saying "Therefore what God has joined together, let no one separate" (10:9). On their own, these verses send the impression that only men could initiate divorce and that Jesus did not allow it.

Yet both Mark and other New Testament writings displayed more diversity in their social understanding of divorce. The passage above was followed by these verses: "Then in the house the disciples asked him again about this matter. He said to them, 'Whoever divorces his wife and marries another commits adultery against her; and if she divorces her husband and marries another, she commits adultery" (10:10–12). Instead of simply prohibiting divorce, these verses suggested that divorce accompanied by subsequent remarriage constituted adultery. In doing so, they reinforced the culture's value of a single marriage. The phrases "whoever divorces his wife" and "if she divorces her husband" also reflected the expectation that both men and women could initiate divorce.

The idea that divorce and remarriage was wrong may point to a criticism of elites who used divorce and remarriage for political gain. The Gospels also gave the specific example of Herod, who married his wife, Herodias, after her divorce from his brother, Philip. John the Baptist was said to have criticized the situation and made an enemy of Herodias as a result (Mark 6:17–29; Matt 14:1–12). The story made visible the political influence of a high-ranking woman, as Herodias maneuvered to have John killed. Matthew stated John's objection to the marriage as a matter of law: "It is not lawful for you to have her" (Matt 14:4). But what made the marriage unlawful was not specified. It may have been the notion that remarriage was adultery, as stated in the passages discussed above. It was also possible that John was not disturbed by divorce and remarriage in general but by the marriage of one's brother's wife (see Lev 18:16, 20).[40] In either case, John's criticism of Herod also reflected common ideals of loyalty within marriage and self-control as a characteristic of good leadership (see chapter 3).

The Gospels were not identical in their teachings on divorce but reflected a variety of views. Matthew's version of this story was similar to Mark's, but it mentioned only the husband as the one who might initiate divorce (Matt 5:31–32; 19:3–9). However, Matthew also suggested that divorce and remarriage were allowed in the case of adultery (19:9). Although Matthew and Mark were similar in many ways, they also showed a variety of opinions on the matter of divorce, each of which resonated in some way with wider cultural views.

Paul's discussion in 1 Cor 7 also conveyed the expectation that men or women could initiate divorce. His instructions to those who were married to unbelievers included both scenarios: if the nonbelieving spouse consented, "he should not divorce her" (7:12), and "she should not divorce him" (7:13). However, Paul did not make a blanket prohibition of divorce. "If the unbelieving partner separates, let it be so; in such a case the brother or sister is not bound" (7:15). Paul assumed that divorce by both men and women was a common phenomenon. His preference throughout the chapter was for believers to remain in their current marital state (7:17–20), but he conceded that both marriage and divorce were necessary in some cases.

Widows

The New Testament texts represented a range of experiences that women had as widows. Some widows were wealthy. Many were poor. Some were highly regarded by their communities. Others were criticized as lazy or immodest. The New Testament writings reflected this variety in the experiences of widows and in the cultural assumptions about widowhood.

Anna (Luke 2:36–38) was an example of a virtuous widow. She was loyal: both devoted to God and faithful to one husband. Her religious piety came through in the description of her: "She never left the temple but worshipped there with fasting and prayer night and day" (2:37). Her piety included religious authority, for she was also known as a "prophet" (v. 36). The story included Anna's marital situation: she was married seven years and she remained a widow until the point when she met the infant Jesus, when she was eighty-four years old. Luke drew on cultural assumptions about the virtuous widow to affirm Anna as a trustworthy religious figure who recognized Jesus through prophetic insight. Neither Anna's stature nor her speech was surprising. The cultural norms about widows were a part of what qualified her to deliver a prophetic message.

The stories of the widow with the coin (Mark 12:41–44; cf. Luke 21:1–4) and the distribution of food to widows in Acts 6:1–6 highlighted the poverty of some widows. In Mark, Jesus extolled the virtue of the widow who gave her only coin to the temple treasury. She was clearly a poor person, whose small gift amounted to all she had. Early readers of the story would likely have been familiar with such poverty among some widows. Similarly, Acts 6 mentioned widows as the recipients of a daily distribution of food, suggesting their need. Complaints about the neglect of some widows led to the election of seven new leaders. The story implied that the community provided daily food for widows as a means of relief.

It can be difficult to tell if some women in New Testament stories were widows or if their husbands were simply not mentioned. Jesus healed Simon Peter's mother-in-law, who was sick with a fever at Simon's house (Mark 1:29–31; Matt 8:14–15; Luke 4:38–39). As the mother of a married daughter, Simon's mother-in-law was of an age when many women were widows. She may have come to live with her daughter on a permanent basis. However, other possibilities cannot be ruled out: she may have traveled to visit her daughter, leaving her husband at home; she may have shared an adjoining part of the house with her husband. Although her widowhood seems likely given her age, there were many instances in which husbands were simply not mentioned.

First Timothy 5 reflected a number of social conventions about widows. First, widows were due honor (5:3). The word "honor" in these verses referred to the respect due to one's elders and also, more concretely, to the financial support that was expected of children.[41]

The letter to Timothy also drew on social conventions of ideal widowhood in its depiction of "real widows" (1 Tim 5:3–16). As in the culture at large, this text portrayed virtuous widows as devoted to God, praying night and day (5:5). They were also loyal to their husbands, shown through having had only one husband (5:9). These virtuous widows were also industrious. The life of the married woman was a training ground in industry and responsible citizenship. Thus, the enrolled widow "must be well attested for her good works, as one who had brought up children, shown hospitality, washed the saints' feet, helped the afflicted, and devoted herself to doing good in every way" (5:11). The widow had status in part because she had already been a productive, married woman.

As in the culture at large, the New Testament also drew on feminine virtues to criticize or warn against certain actions. First Timothy 5 pointed to the danger that young widows might not learn the virtue of industry and therefore become idle (5:13). Many interpreters have asserted that this language pointed to the behavior of actual women in the community who were teaching in ways they should not.[42] This interpretation would be more persuasive if the accusation were not so conventional. Both the virtues and the potential vices here were statements of familiar cultural norms. Because of this, these verses were less likely a description of the behavior of actual women and more likely the use of conventional virtues to motivate exemplary behavior.

Similarly, the desire for younger widows to marry (5:14) reflected the assumption that marriage cultivated the virtues of modesty, industry, and loyalty. But the preference for marriage should not be taken as a mandate that was imposed upon all women.[43] Many women likely could not remarry. Those who could probably saw it as an opportunity to increase their social status and influence, and not as something restrictive. Marriage was a place to gain social influence through a good match and the responsibility of managing the household. For wealthier women, who were more likely to be able to remarry, a second marriage would bring additional social influence and status.

Chapter 5

Class Status, Wealth, and Patronage

ALTHOUGH ANCIENT WOMEN WERE WIDELY considered socially inferior to men, social status was a complex mix of factors. A number of elements contributed to one's social status, including family of origin, wealth, citizenship, gender, and one's standing as a slave, freed, or free-born person. Of these, gender was by no means the most important. Although it is common to think of ancient women as being socially inferior to men, in this chapter I describe a variety of factors that determined social status as a way of explaining the social influence women exercised in this period.

Elite families in Rome and other cities were of high status. In Rome, the equestrian or senatorial orders governed the city during the Republican period. In the Imperial period their legislative powers were more limited, but they still held political appointments in Rome, provincial government, and the military. Being a descendant of a senatorial or equestrian family was one marker of status. In the provinces, local elite families functioned in similar ways.

Wealth was a major contributor to social status in the Imperial period. Wealth and family status often coincided, but there was some movement in and out of the elite social ranks, driven primarily by gain or loss of wealth. Rich people built temples and baths and beautified their cities with monuments. They were chosen as magistrates and religious leaders, in part because their wealth allowed them to sponsor the festivals and games that were an essential part of the life and prestige of the city. People with this level of wealth could often influence the local politics in their town and could act as advocates for their family's interests or for the interests of their clients.

Citizenship was also a factor in social status. People were citizens of a particular city rather than a country. If a married couple were citizens, then their children were born citizens of that city as well. Citizenship could also be granted by city officials as a way of honoring a noncitizen for contributions to the city. The emperor bestowed Roman citizenship on many people of high status in the provinces as a way of encouraging cooperation with Rome. During the first and second centuries, the number of people outside of Rome who held Roman citizenship gradually increased until the emperor Caracalla granted citizenship to all free persons in the year 212.

Another factor in social rank was a person's status as freeborn, freed, or enslaved. Freeborn people had higher status than free people who had been slaves and were manumitted by their masters. Slaves who were formally manumitted became both free people and Roman citizens. They did not break ties with their masters, however, but remained connected in a patron-client relationship. Slaves could not be citizens of Rome, nor could citizens become slaves. If Roman individuals were captured and enslaved, they would lose their Roman citizenship, at least temporarily, for a citizen could not be a slave. Free persons had legal and social rights that slaves did not have.

Modern readers may expect that slaves were of lower social status than citizens in the Roman period. Although this was generally true, the status of slaves varied a great deal, depending on who their master was and the tasks they were assigned. Slaves played managerial as well as menial roles, and some slaves were trusted by their masters and held positions of authority. Slaves could own property under a legal condition in which they were granted this property by the master. Because of this practice, some slaves of high-ranking people became very wealthy themselves and exercised considerable social influence. Although they were slaves, their wealth and access to a powerful master gave them influence greater than that experienced by some freeborn people of lesser means.

Gender also contributed to social status. Men had higher status than women and accordingly had greater social influence. However, any of these other factors might give a woman relatively greater social standing than a man. A highborn or wealthy woman would have greater status than a poor man, a freeborn woman than a male slave, and so forth.

Each of these categories of status had a clearly defined hierarchy. Men were perceived as better than women, free people outranked slaves, and people of high birth were superior to those from less well-known families. The assignment of status according to these categories is visible in many sources in the historical record.

However, most people embodied a mixture of the categories. One person might be a freedwoman with citizenship. She would outrank a male slave, even though she was female. If that slave was a person of great wealth, however, that could turn the tables in his favor. A highborn woman would have outranked a citizen male with no noble heritage. A wealthy freedman was more influential than a poor freeborn person.

This variability in social rank helps to explain some of the evidence of women's participation in the social and political arenas. When other aspects of social status were equal, women were deemed to be of lower standing than men. However, some women had high social status relative to those around them. For example, a woman who was not elite but was a freeborn Roman citizen might outrank a man who was less wealthy, enslaved, or a foreigner.

WEALTH

The first and second centuries were a time of relative prosperity across the empire. There were certainly great disparities between the highest and lowest economic levels. Classicist Willem

Jongman estimated that a subsistence level income was 115 sesterces per year, while the annual income of Pliny the Younger was
1.2 million sesterces. But many people on the lower end of the economic spectrum also lived above the subsistence level. Jongman
argued that evidence like the base pay for soldiers or the price of
slaves reflected wage levels that were higher than subsistence. This
income pattern was also supported by levels of consumption. He
concluded, "Even many ordinary citizens were moderately prosperous, and there were also many moderately wealthy people in
between the masses of modest means and the rich but small political elite. Moreover, together they enjoyed the benefits of public
expenditure on such things as roads, harbors, aqueducts, baths,
market buildings, public distributions, and much more."[1] Rome
had relatively high per capita incomes compared to other pre-
industrial economies.

Women and men benefited from the prosperity of this era.
Classicist Richard Saller estimated that women owned one third
of property at this time. This figure suggests that while women
wore not the equals of men in terms of ownership and wealth,
women's ownership of property was a familiar part of the landscape of Roman culture. Evidence comes from a variety of sources
and suggests patterns of property ownership among elite and
nonelite women.

Some women of the elite classes owned vast estates. Cicero
wrote about his wife, Terentia, selling a row of houses to support
the family during his exile (*Fam.* 8). Pliny the Younger described
properties owned by his mother-in-law, Pompeia Celerina (*Ep.*
1.4; 6.10; cf. 3.19). Inscriptions attested the wealth of Ummidia
Quadratilla, who built an amphitheater and temple and restored a
theater in her home town of Casinum (*CIL* 10.5183, *AE* 1992.244).
Pliny also mentioned her in a letter in which he praised her rearing
of her grandson, although he was critical of her luxurious lifestyle
(*Ep.* 7.24). Much of the evidence for the wealth of such women
became visible in their generous use of it through patronage—
those who, like Ummidia Quadratilla, donated buildings and

entertainment, or served in civic and religious offices. (See the section on Patronage in this chapter.)

Sub-elite women also owned property, sometimes in large amounts. Eumachia was a woman from a wealthy local family in Pompeii. In the first century, she funded a grand building bordering the forum of the city. The building contained a statue of Eumachia (see figure 5.1) and two dedicatory inscriptions: "Eumachia, daughter of Lucius, public priestess, in her own name and that of her son, Marcus Numistrius Fronto, built at her own expense the *chalcidicum*, crypt and portico in honor of Augustan Concord

FIGURE 5.1 Statue of Eumachia. Museo Archeologico Nazionale. Photo: Alinari/Art Resource, NY. Used by permission.

and Piety and also dedicated them" (*CIL* 10.810, 811).[2] Many similar inscriptions honored women in the Latin West for their contributions to their cities or to civic groups.[3]

In Asia Minor and Egypt, similar patterns of property owner-ship emerge from inscriptions and papyri. Like their counterparts in Italy, women in Asia Minor donated buildings and adorned their cities with statues and monuments. For example, Menodora, a woman from a small city called Sillyon in southern Asia Minor, was from a prominent local family who were not Roman citi-zens. Inscriptions in her city suggest that Menodora spent around 1 million *denarii* in benefactions to her city.[4] Transactions re-garding women's property also emerge from papyri in Egypt. One Egyptian woman petitioned the local ruler to purchase properties that were adjacent to land that she or her daughter already owned (*P.Turner* 24).

Inscriptions and papyri also give glimpses of poorer women's property ownership. One divorce agreement recorded the re-turn of a dowry: "Zois acknowledges that she has received from Antipatros by hand from his house clothes to the value of one hundred and twenty drachmas and a pair of gold earrings, which he received as a dowry" (*BGU* 4.1103).[5] Another marriage contract recorded the transmission of a modest dowry, consisting of 200 silver drachmas, jewelry, and household utensils (*P.Mich.* 2.121 recto 4.1). Although the monetary value of the dowry is small, the legal form it took was similar to the dowries of other women with great wealth. Another woman registered her ownership of six camels, which were an economic asset in her city at the edge of the desert (*P.Grenf.* 2.45a). Such documents show the extent and frequency of women's property ownership and the everyday transactions that they undertook.

Jewish women also owned property in varying amounts. First-century historian Josephus wrote of the great wealth of Queen Shelamzion (Alexandria), who ruled Judea from 75 to 67 B.C.E. (Josephus, *Ant.* 13.418), and of Berenice, the daughter of Herod Agrippa (*Ant.* 20.146). Although fictional, the apocryphal story of Judith assumed the reader would be familiar with the wealth of a woman like Judith, who inherited land, livestock, and slaves from her husband (Jud 8:7).

Similarly, among nonelite Jewish women, papyrus records show property ownership of land and other items. One papyrus recorded the gift from Salome Grapte to her daughter, Salome Komaïse, of a date orchard along with the rights to water it (*P. XHev/Se* gr 64). The papers of Babatha (see also chapter 4) included a registration of her property and a record of a loan to her husband Judah (*P.Yadin* 16, 17). Thus, property ownership was not restricted to a few women with great wealth but was part of the everyday lives of women and men across the Mediterranean.

Women's property ownership also included their ownership of slaves. Elite households displayed their wealth through large numbers of slaves. Some women brought household slaves with them in marriage as part of their property. Their ownership of slaves was reflected in the writings of elite men. For example, Juvenal satirized the wealthy matron who beat her slaves at the slightest provocation (*Sat.* 6.480–495). Slaves of elite women also showed up in papyrus records as part of business and legal transactions. One such papyrus recorded a managerial slave acting on behalf of an elite Roman woman, Antonia (*P.Oxy.* 2.244).

But it was not only the elite who owned slaves in this period. Many people did, including those with modest wealth. Many fictional stories mentioned women owning slaves, assuming that readers were familiar with the practice. For example, Petronius's *Satyricon* included the story of a woman traveling on a ship and mentioned in passing her *ancillae*, or female slaves (*Sat.* 105). In addition to such literary works, papyri and inscriptions recorded social practices involving actual slaves. Some documented the purchase or sale of slaves by female owners (e.g., *P.Oxy.* 2.375). Slave owners sometimes freed their slaves, either as a reward for years of service or because the slave or another party paid for their release. Papyri record both women and men undertaking these actions. One has an account of a woman owner freeing a female slave (*P.Oxy.* 38.2843). In another, a sister and brother freed their slave, a Jewish woman, after receiving payment from "the community of the Jews" (*CPJ* 473). The author of a second-century Christian work, the Shepherd of Hermas, wrote that he was at one time sold to a woman named Rhoda (*Vis.* 1.1).

Inscriptions point to complex relationships between slaves or freed slaves and their masters or patrons. For example, Junia Libertas of Ostia, a wealthy but not elite woman, recorded her gift of the rights to a block of buildings and shops to her freedmen and women and their descendants.[6] A study by Ilse Muller has shown the common pattern of widows being commemorated in funerary inscriptions by their freedpersons or slaves.[7]

PATRONAGE

Patron-client relationships pervaded Roman society. People sought patrons of higher social status who could influence others on their behalf. Patrons often wrote letters of introduction for their clients who traveled to other cities where the patron had connections. A patron might also have arranged a business partnership or recommended someone for a political appointment. They might have approached another family regarding the marriage of one of the client's children. Patrons also made loans and bequests to their clients or guaranteed a loan the client received from another source. Thus, the relationships between patrons and clients touched many aspects of life.

Patronage was therefore an important form of leadership during this period. Even when they held no office or title, patrons were people with influence in their communities. Although cultural norms limited women's participation as voters in assemblies, many modes of political influence were available to both men and women. In a treatise about whether older men should still participate in politics, Plutarch argued that it was unseemly for older men to hold on to offices or make too many speeches (*An seni* 794). However, they should not remove themselves completely but should work behind the scenes (*An seni* 795). He argued that statesmanship did not only consist in "ranting round the speakers' platform proposing laws and making motions." Instead, the statesman "is always acting as a statesman by urging those on who have power, guiding those who need guidance, assisting those who are deliberating, reforming those who act wrongly, encouraging those who are right-minded" (*An seni* 796).[8] Plutarch had in mind the elite males of Greek and Roman cities. But the avenues of civic power that he named as "statesmanship" were also available to others, and the evidence suggests that women participated in these ways. A patron's connections to powerful people made it possible for that person to assist in the social, political, and economic advancement of others. Clients owed allegiance to their patrons, and the patron could call upon the client for various kinds of service.

Many patrons led in official capacities as well, and their titles were recorded in inscriptions. In Greek inscriptions, offices such as *stephanophoros* and *demiourgos* designated the city magistrate. Other titles like *archiereus* served priestly functions. However, religious and civic functions overlapped to a large extent. People understood the gods to be protectors of the city, and so religion functioned in part to maintain the safety and status of the city. The stephanophoros might have made sacrifices on behalf of the city at the beginning of a religious festival. The priest of the city's chief god or goddess likewise held a civic office.[9]

People in all levels of society participated as patrons. Wealthier people donated buildings and monuments, served as magistrates and religious officials, and financed civic and religious festivals and games. A nonelite person might have been a patron of an association or guild, donating a meeting room or items to the group. Even lower-status free people served as patrons by making small loans or gifts. People of these varying status levels also sought the patronage of a person with higher status and so were both patron and client in different settings.

Because people of various social classes owned slaves, they would serve as patron to their freed slaves as well. The freedperson remained in a relationship with the former owner, who became the patron of the freedman or freedwoman. Freedpeople often worked for their patron in a capacity similar to what they did as slaves. Thus, manumission was not the termination of the slave-owner relationship but an important piece of an ongoing, hierarchical relationship.

Both men and women served as patrons in similar capacities. Groups and individuals sought a person of high social status to be their patron, regardless of gender. As Carolyn Osiek wrote, "In the Roman world, status was always more important than gender; that is, higher social status always took preeminence over the sex of the persons involved. Thus in the highly developed system of patronage and benefaction, women were actively engaged at every level."[10] Women also pursued honor and asserted their influence through patronage.

The patronage of the empress, Livia, wife of Octavian, set a standard of generosity that other women in the empire emulated. She received petitioners in her home and made extensive gifts to the populace as well as to individuals.[11] She dedicated a shrine to the goddess Concordia, who represented both marital and political harmony.[12] Livia's acts of patronage gave her a visible role in the empire. Other women in the provinces mimicked Livia's civic role, although without the vast wealth that she had at her disposal.[13]

Such patronage brought political influence as well as social prestige. Bernice (or Berenice), the daughter of Herod Agrippa I, was an elite Jewish woman whose influence was noted in literary sources. When the emperor Vespasian rose to power following a year of turmoil after Nero's death in 68 C.E., Bernice and other local leaders supported him by recognizing his reign with lavish gifts (Tacitus, *Hist.* 2.81). In giving such gifts leaders like Bernice sought to commend themselves to the new ruler. But the gifts also aided Vespasian's consolidation of power through the recognition of his office. The historian Josephus also described Bernice's attempts to intervene in the rising tensions that led to the Jewish war of 68–70 C.E. Although she was unsuccessful in this case, her efforts were the kinds of actions that were expected of a person of her stature.

Women in Italy and the provinces also exercised influence as patrons. They held civic and religious offices, and they donated buildings, entertainment, and meals. One example from Misenum in Italy commemorated the generosity of Cassia Victoria:

> Cassia Victoria, daughter of Gaius, priestess of the Augustales, dedicated in her own name and in that of her husband, Lucius Laecanius Primitivus, a pronaos with columns and epistyle, because of [the Augustales'] extraordinary good will towards them. She gave a banquet and to each man twelve sesterces. (*AE* 1993.477)[14]

The inscription to Cassia Victoria fit a pattern of civic generosity known in other inscriptions honoring both men and women. The inscriptions often accompanied statues, which were commissioned by the city to honor generous donors. Cassia Victoria was a priestess of the Augustales, which was a priestly order responsible for the worship of the emperor. She built a portion of the shrine in her city and gave a banquet to celebrate its dedication.

Inscriptions like this point to the social power of women like Cassia Victoria. Modern readers should recognize that such inscriptions are like the tip of an iceberg. The words remaining form the visible part, but "underneath" and not visible to us now was the social status and influence that the people honored in the inscription had in their community. The inscribed words came about because of the acts the individual undertook to bring honor to the city by contributing to its adornment and financing civic festivals. The donor of such costly items was a person of high status. Inscriptions like these added to the status and influence of donors by publicly honoring them through this declaration of their deeds. The inscriptions remaining allow us a glimpse of the influence these patrons had.

Many inscriptions in Greece also attested to the various roles women played as patrons in their communities. One example from the mid-first century was Junia Theodora of Corinth. Five inscriptions praised Junia for her acts as a patron to the people of

Lycia. These notices honored Junia for her generosity, hospitality, and advocacy on behalf of the people. For example, one decree by the Lycian assembly hailed Junia Theodora for her "zeal and generosity to the nation" and for having "secured the friendship of many leaders for the nation."[15] Junia exerted her influence to gain support for the Lycian people in a time of political turmoil. Another inscription with similar content made it clear that Junia welcomed some who were in exile for political reasons, and it declared her to be generous and loyal. The assembly sent her a crown of gold as a gift.[16]

Another example comes from Perge in Asia Minor. Plankia Magna was an important benefactor and leader of the city. Inscriptions found there name many of her offices, including demiourgos (a civic title with some religious functions) and priestess of Artemis, the city's most important deity (*AE* 1958.78). (See figure 5.2). Plankia Magna donated a large gate complex and an arch to beautify her city. The gate complex included many statues honoring the gods and important people from the

FIGURE 5.2 Plancia Magna dedicatory inscription, Perge. Photo: Carolyn Osiek. Used by permission.

city. Statues of her father and brother were among the civic figures. They are interesting because her relatives are identified as "father of Plankia Magna" and "brother of Plankia Magna."[17] While modern readers may expect ancient women to be identified by their male relatives, the reverse was the case here. The identification through relationship with Plankia Magna suggests her stature and importance as the donor of the project and reminds us that women also sought and gained honor through such acts of generosity.

Many women in Asia Minor held these civic and religious offices. They were magistrates like stephanophoros and demiourgos. They were priests of the imperial cult, as well as of other gods and goddesses, both major and minor. They held titles like "mother of the city" and "daughter of the city," which conveyed their status and prestige. Although women occupied a narrower range of offices and appeared less frequently in inscriptions than men, many of the titles attributed to them were the same ones men held.

As these examples make clear, women's patronage had political as well as social effects. Junia Theodora's patronage of the Lycian people included offering them a refuge in a time of political turmoil. She offered not only hospitality but the political sponsorship that the Lycians needed. Titles held by others like Plankia Magna and Cassia Victoria pointed to the political influence of these women. The titles conveyed a high degree of honor and specified a civic function in festivals or rites. This status meant such women would be highly sought after as patrons and were in a position to advocate for the interests of others as well as their own interests.

The second-century Christian work, the Acts of Thecla, reflected the social influence patrons held in this period. In the second part of the story, Thecla was condemned to the beasts. A wealthy woman, Tryphaena, offered Thecla protection in her home until the games began. Tryphaena was identified as a "queen" (*basilissa*, *ATh* 27, 28, 36), a regional title found in other inscriptions.[18] Tryphaena's social status ultimately brought the games to an end, enabling Thecla's release (*ATh* 36–37).

Inscriptions also identified Jewish women with titles like head of the synagogue and elder. For example, one second-century inscription from Smyrna read: "Rufina, a Jew, head of the synagogue, built this tomb for her freed slaves and the slaves raised in her house. No one else has the right to bury anyone [here]. If someone should dare to do, he or she will pay 1,400 *denars* to the sacred treasury and 1,000 *denars* to the Jewish people. A copy of this inscription has been placed in the [public] archives" (*CIJ* 1.741).[19] Other inscriptions commemorated donations, both large and small. One woman gave an entire building (*CIJ* 1.766). Others donated a portion of a mosaic floor. For example: "Saprikia made 150 feet [of the mosaic], in fulfillment of a vow, for the salvation of all (her) relatives" (*CIJ* 1.811).[20] The scattered evidence suggests that Jewish women played roles as patrons and leaders of Jewish organizations similar to those of non-Jewish women in their civic and religious groups.

Women of varying class levels made loans and bequests, forms of patronage in which men also participated. Large loans by wealthy women were seen in literary sources. Cicero wrote of money he owed to Ovia (*Att.* 12.21.5 [*LCL* 260]) and Caerellia (*Att.* 12.51.3 [*LCL* 296]). Pliny the Younger spoke of borrowing from his mother-in-law, Pompeia Celerina, whose properties were mentioned above (*Ep.* 3.19). Assessing the activities of women from the evidence of Pompeii, Jane Gardner argued that in matters of personal business, women and men undertook similar roles in granting and receiving loans. She noted, however, that "women are not found in any of our texts guaranteeing other people's debts."[21] The preference for men in this role showed the cultural bias in favor of male patrons and suggests that social practices may have excluded women from some acts of patronage. Yet there were also great similarities in the actions of male and female patrons.

Smaller bequests and loans show similar activity among nonelite women. In one papyrus, two sisters borrowed 372 drachmas from another, wealthier woman (*P.Kron.* 17). Another document recorded a loan of 3,500 drachmas by Isidora to Tamestha (*P.Tebt.* 2.389). Wax tablets from areas near Pompeii enumerated loans of varying sizes with women as both creditors and debtors.[22]

Because women were owners of slaves, they also manumitted slaves and became patrons of their freed slaves.[23] Inscriptions like that of Junia Libertas, cited above, showed the generosity of some patrons to their freedpeople. Libertas donated the income from a large building complex to her freed people and their descendants, with the expectation that they would carry out yearly sacrifices in her honor. Other inscriptions from slaves or freedpeople praised their master or patron for their benevolence: "To Lalla of Arneae, daughter of Timarchus son of Diotimus, Masas, who was set free by her, set this up in accordance with her will" (*Pleket* 14).[24] Such inscriptions showed the patronage relationship from a different angle, the honor due the patron from the client.

These activities of nonelite women suggest a cultural pattern in which such women also exercised patronage. They did not have access to the highest circles of power, but they sought honor in ways that were accessible to them. By gaining honor, they accumulated social influence which they employed in various ways.

SUMMARY

Women owned property and accumulated wealth. Like men, they put their wealth to work for the sake of their families, friends, and communities. In doing so they accrued the honor that was due to patrons. Although their wealth was a smaller proportion than that owned by men and they appeared less frequently as patrons, the evidence suggests that they acted in many of the same capacities that men did. They managed their property and exercised the offices in which they served. People in the community honored those who held high social positions, and this honor translated into forms of social and political power, for women as well as men.

WEALTH AND PATRONAGE IN THE NEW TESTAMENT

The language of the New Testament reflects the cultural norms of women's property ownership and patronage. The New Testament writings were not legal documents addressing property ownership as a subject. But women's ownership and management of property sometimes became visible in these texts. The language assumed that ancient readers shared a context in which such actions were a familiar feature of society. If modern readers understand that women could own property and serve as patrons, we may notice them doing so in the New Testament. Likewise, if we do not assume all women were inferior to all men, we may notice women with significant social and political influence.

Property Ownership and Management

Women in the New Testament owned property in varying amounts. The widow's offering of two copper coins (Mark 12:41–44; Luke 21:1–4) represented the lower end of the economic spectrum while also indicating that the coins belonged to this woman. The parable of a woman who owned ten silver coins and lost one (Luke 15:8–10) was another text that assumed women were owners of property. Martha, who welcomed Jesus into her home and offered hospitality to him (Luke 10:38), likely did so from her own resources. These passages did not convey that women's property ownership was unusual or suspect, but presented it as a regular part of the landscape of ancient life.

Some signs of greater wealth also appeared in the New Testament. The woman who anointed Jesus (e.g., Mark 14:3–9) expended a large amount of money in doing so. It is impossible to tell what the woman's social status was on the basis of the passage. She may not have been a wealthy person, but the value of her gift ("three hundred denarii," Mark 14:5) suggested some accumulation of wealth. Similarly, the author of 1 Timothy warned against types of adornment used to signify one's wealth, including braided hair, gold, pearls, and expensive clothes (1 Tim 2:9). Although the earliest Christians did not come from the elite classes, like other people in the period some were fairly prosperous. Women as well as men were owners of this wealth.

New Testament texts also reflected cultural expectations regarding women's decision making about property. The author of 1 Timothy expected that a virtuous widow had been active as a manager of her household: "She must be well attested for her good works, as one who has brought up children, shown hospitality, washed the saints' feet, helped the afflicted, and devoted herself to doing good in every way" (1 Tim 5:10). The letter did not attempt to clarify whether the woman was using her own financial resources toward these ends or managing those of her husband. Culturally, either one could have been the case. The woman was described as actively pursuing these ends. Her actions were not only allowed but they were also virtuous.

The story of Ananias and Sapphira's deception in Acts 5 also reflected the joint nature of marital decision making regarding property. Ananias and Sapphira's actions were intertwined. "A man named Ananias, with the consent of his wife Sapphira, sold a piece of property; with his wife's knowledge, he kept back some of the proceeds, and brought only a part and laid it at the apostles' feet" (Acts 5:1–2). Acts described Ananias as the actor in the sale of the property, but his wife Sapphira consented, both to the sale of the property and to the deception of holding back a portion of the proceeds. Peter accused them of having "agreed together" to put the Lord to the test (5:9). The passage made sense in light of the value placed on a couple's ability to make joint decisions even though property was not jointly held. (See the discussion of marriage in chapter 4.)

Patronage

Women shared in the social expectation that property owners would use their wealth for the benefit of the community. Like women in the culture at large, New Testament women sponsored individuals and religious movements through the donation of money and meeting spaces. They also asserted their social influence to affect those who made political decisions.

Women's patronage and influence in the early Christian movement appear in a number of passages. One brief example occurs in the greetings at the end of Paul's letter to the Romans: "I commend to you our sister Phoebe, a deacon of the church at Cenchreae, so that you may welcome her in the Lord as is fitting for the saints, and help her in whatever she may require from you, for she has been a benefactor of many and of myself as well" (Romans 16:1–2). Paul commended Phoebe, a deacon from Cenchrae, the city which, paired with Corinth, was a major conduit of travel between the Adriatic and Aegean seas. Phoebe was traveling to Rome, and Paul asked that the Roman church help her with anything she needed.

Paul used two words in describing Phoebe that point to her patronage. The first was "deacon" (v. 1; Greek, *diakonos*). Phoebe's leadership in the church is sometimes obscured through the English translation of this word as "servant" instead of "deacon" (see, for example, the King James Version or New American Standard Bible). Although "servant" is one possible meaning of this word, it is also a term for an official of a religious group. Furthermore, Paul used the same word in Phil 1:1 to hail the leaders of the church at Philippi. Introducing Phoebe as "deacon of the church at Cenchreae" similarly indicated that she served in an official capacity. In the later church, deacons took on regular roles in baptism and service at the Lord's Supper, and there were many inscriptions and church documents that referred to women as deacons.[25] However, in this early period, it is difficult to tell what a deacon's specific roles were, and it is likely that the role varied from place to place. Although we cannot say for certain what Phoebe's job description was, the terminology Paul used identified her as a leader of the church in her city.

Paul also introduced Phoebe as a "benefactor" (Rom 16:2; Greek, *prostatis*), a patron who looked out for the interests of her clients. The language assumed a social context in which women played important roles as protectors and advocates for others.

Paul indicated Phoebe had played this role "for many," including Paul himself (v. 2). Junia Theodora, whose inscriptions were cited above, provides an interesting parallel because she was a contemporary of Paul and Phoebe and came from the neighboring city of Corinth. Although Junia was an elite woman and Roman citizen, her inscriptions remind us that the patronage of women was not unusual at this time, and that women with status were sought as patrons of various groups. Traveling to Rome, Phoebe should likely be viewed as the bearer of Paul's letter and an official delegate from her church.

The Gospel of Luke also indicated that a number of women traveled with Jesus and supported his ministry. The Gospel names three of them, Mary Magdalene, Susanna, and Joanna, the wife of Herod's steward Chuza (8:1–3). Jesus had healed these women and they "provided for them out of their resources" (8:3). The language reinforces the idea that the women possessed their own resources and used them in service to the Jesus movement. In its cultural context, this was an act of patronage.

The New Testament also conveys the influence of women in political settings. Herodias found an opportunity for revenge against a political enemy, John the Baptist, and asked Herod for his head (Mark 6:17–29; Matt 14:1–12). Herodias was not the one with formal judicial power, but the story assumed that the kind of influence she exercised would be familiar to its readers. The story portrayed Herod as a weak ruler guided by his passions rather than self-control. He put himself in a bind by making a promise that he would not otherwise wish to keep (Mark 6:26; Matt 14:9). Herodias seized on the opportunity to take action against her political enemy.

In another example, Matthew's version of the trial of Jesus portrayed the influence of Pilate's wife when she sent Pilate word about a dream she had of Jesus's innocence (Matt 27:19). Although her words did not affect the outcome of the trial, the story was part of the way the author underscored Jesus's innocence. In telling such a story without explanation or apology, the narrative also conveyed that such intervention by a high-status woman was plausible.

One further story involving the influence and status of women is seen in Acts 25. When Porcius Festus took over from Felix as the Roman procurator, the local ruler, King Agrippa, came with his sister Bernice to welcome Festus (Acts 25:13). Festus told the king about Paul, and the king agreed to give him a hearing. "So on the next day Agrippa and Bernice came with great pomp, and they entered the audience hall with the military tribunes and the prominent men of the city" (25:23). Upon hearing Paul, they responded positively. The author again mentioned Bernice and those seated with her as saying, "This man is doing nothing to deserve death or imprisonment" (26:31). As in the sources mentioned above, in Acts, Bernice is presumed to be a powerful, elite woman whose presence would be noteworthy. Although Bernice was not the person with the formal, legal power to decide Paul's fate, she had the political status to influence those who did, if she chose to use her power in that way.

All of these examples underscore the influence of women patrons. The patrons had different levels of social status, but they used their standing to influence the events around them and to support groups or individuals. The New Testament reflected cultural practices by which patrons exercised leadership of various kinds in their communities. Some held official titles and exercised their offices. In many cases, men and women shared similar titles and official functions. Other roles of patrons involved using resources and status on behalf of others. The New Testament suggests that both men and women participated in these roles in the early church.

Chapter 6

Occupations

WOMEN IN THE NEW TESTAMENT period performed a variety of tasks and occupations. The evidence that remains suggests that women had a narrower range of occupations available to them than men did. They were less likely to hold high managerial posts or political offices. Nevertheless, women performed valuable labor in this period.

In addition to their management of household resources and property, many women also worked in business or had various jobs, either as free women or as slaves. The evidence of their employment often comes from inscriptions, where they or a family member proclaimed their occupation. Other evidence comes from literary sources and, in a few cases, pictures of women carved in funeral reliefs. These sources expressed no surprise regarding these women's work, suggesting that such jobs were an ordinary part of the social landscape.

Inscriptions recorded a number of jobs that women did. Although we often know nothing else of the life of the woman mentioned, the fact that her occupation was recognized suggests that it was a part of her identity. Inscriptions were a means of honoring the living and memorializing the dead, and mentioning a woman's occupation seems to have been a way both of attributing honor and remembering her. For example: "Sacred to the gods of the dead. To Hapate, a Greek stenographer, who lived 25 years. Pittosus put this up for his sweetest wife" (*CIL* 6.33892 [*ILS* 7760]).[1] Pittosus remembered Hapate in part through commemorating her occupation.

MOTHERHOOD AND RAISING CHILDREN

I include motherhood in this chapter because it was work and because it occupied a portion of many women's time. Parenting was not exclusively a female role, nor was it likely to be a woman's sole occupation. Women were involved in the economic productivity of their households, whether as managers of slaves and freedpeople or as laborers themselves—and, often, as both. Yet women were often responsible for managing a child's education and rearing alongside these other tasks.

Women were the primary caretakers of young children, either as mothers or as wet nurses and nannies. The care and early education of children was viewed as the mother's responsibility. Wealthier women hired others to do many of the tasks of childrearing or put their slaves to work on these tasks. Thus, many women were also involved in caring for children who were not their own.

Childbearing and Contraception

Scholars have estimated that to maintain the population as a whole, every woman would need to give birth to five or six children on average. This average number was high because the infant and child mortality rate was quite substantial. Before reaching age one, 25 to 30 percent of infants died, and child mortality continued to be high until age five. Because population numbers seem to have been relatively stable, pregnancy and childbirth must have been a regular part of most women's lives.[2]

Childbearing was an expected outcome of marriage. Literary sources reinforced the notion that a goal of marriage was the production of children. Furthermore, Latin marriage documents from Egypt stated that the marriage was "for the sake of producing children."[3] Augustus's marriage laws (see chapter 4) rewarded men and women who produced three or four children. These parents gained status and could inherit a greater proportion of their spouse's property.

The expectation to produce children during marriage did not mean that childbirth outside of marriage was uncommon or frowned upon. Children born outside of marriage could not be the legitimate heirs of the father under Roman law. However, there were many reasons that women conceived and bore children outside of marriage in ways that were considered socially acceptable. Elite Roman men might form relationships to women whom they could not marry for social reasons. Soldiers were forbidden to marry during service but often had families that were simply not recognized by marriage. Such relationships were not necessarily viewed as immoral. They might be long term, affectionate partnerships, but their offspring could not enjoy the legal status of an heir.

Slave women also gave birth in a variety of situations. They were sexually available to their masters and might bear a child as a result. Slaves could also be paired together, or allowed to pair, in order to produce more slaves for the household. Regardless of paternity, the child of a slave woman was born a slave. In the first and second centuries, when Rome did not add many slaves through conquest of new territories, the birth of slave children was one of the main ways the slave population was maintained.

Some women took steps to limit or terminate pregnancies. Contraceptive substances were known at this time, although there was also a good deal of misinformation.[4] Augustine's laws promoting childbearing did not prevent couples from limiting families. Some sources implied that the upper classes avoided having too many children.[5] One motivation may have been that a father's estate was divided between his children upon his death. To avoid having large estates broken up and diluting the influence of the family, elite parents may have sought to limit the number of children they had. However, the early death of many children would have made the "right" number of children difficult to calculate or maintain.

Nurture and Education of Children

Many ancient sources attest to the labor of breastfeeding and caring for very young children. Nursing one's own offspring was viewed as virtuous. In stories meant to praise, Plutarch mentioned his wife nursing her son at her own breast (*Cons. ux.* 5) and the wife of Cato the Elder doing the same (*Cat. Maj.* 20). One Latin inscription memorialized Graxia Alexandria, praising her modesty (*pudicitia*) and that she "brought up her children at her own breast" (*CIL* 6.19128 [*ILS* 8451]). As with other honorary inscriptions, the description attributed honor to the deceased by citing conventional virtues.

Another kind of evidence comes from a papyrus letter in which a mother berated her son for not writing to her: "Was it for this that I carried you for ten months and nursed you for three years, so that you would be incapable of remembering me by letter?" (*P.Berenike* 2.129).[6] The mother asserted that a virtuous action on her part was not returned by her son. Her words assumed that nursing would serve as evidence of her care for her son.

Yet many sources also attested that hiring a wet nurse was a common practice. Cicero suggested this was standard, at least among elites. Although he asserted that "the seeds of virtue are inborn in our dispositions," Cicero went on to argue that this virtue was quickly corrupted, so that "it seems as if we drank in deception with our nurse's milk" (*Tusc.* 3.1).[7] Cicero's words assumed that a wet nurse was the customary way of providing nourishment to children of his class.

Nursing was commemorated in inscriptions in the same way other jobs of the period were recorded. Latin funerary inscriptions designated a named woman as *nutrix* (nurse) of a particular child.[8] For example, one inscription commemorated a nurse of the imperial family: "Prima, freedwoman of the emperor [Tiberius] and empress [Livia], nurse of Julia [Livilla], daughter of Germanicus" (*CIL* 6.4352).[9] The presence of such inscriptions suggests that wet nursing was a profession that brought honor.

Wet nurses were employed for a variety of reasons, not least of which was the death of the mother in childbirth. There were other reasons as well. The physician Soranus suggested that it might aid a woman's recovery not to breastfeed (Soranus, *Gynecology* 2.11). It was also known that nursing could have a contraceptive effect. One author asserted that women may have hired a wet nurse because they were "in haste to have more children" (Ps.-Plutarch *Lib. ed.* 5). In nonelite families, economic considerations likely played a part in deciding to hire a wet nurse. Some mothers nursed their own children of necessity. But other women's economic contributions to their families may have made the hiring of a wet nurse worthwhile. Some elite male writers portrayed the women's motives as merely selfish. The sophist Favorinus suggested some women did not nurse their children "because they think it disfigures the charms of their beauty" (Aulus Gellius, *Noct. att.* 12.1.8).[10] Selfish motivations were possible, of course, but were certainly not always the case.

Women who worked as wet nurses included slave, freed, and freeborn women. Many sources gave the impression of "hiring" a wet nurse, although this may have involved paying an owner for the use of his or her slave.[11] Numerous contracts for wet nurses are found in papyri, attesting to the paid nature of the work (e.g., *BGU* 4.1058; *CPJ* 146; *P.Mich.* 3.202). Dio Chrysostom's remarks gave the impression that nursing was reputable work for lower-class freeborn women. Dio implied that the work was undertaken as a result of poverty but argued that the occupation itself was honorable (*Ven.* 7.114).

For children, breastfeeding was a source of nourishment, but it was also viewed as part of their early education. The wet nurse also cared for, spoke, and sang to the young child. One author noted the importance of having a Greek-speaking wet nurse (Ps.-Plutarch, *Lib. ed.* 5). Similarly, writing about the proper education of elite males who would be schooled in oratorical skills, Quintillian stressed the importance of engaging a wet nurse who used proper grammar (*Inst.* 1.1.4). In the inscription to Graxia Alexandria, above, the word "brought up," *educare*, suggests more than simple nourishment. Breastfeeding was associated with learning and wisdom. Children learned from their mothers and wet nurses even at a young age.

Children learned more than just grammar from their nurses. Tacitus attributed the decline in oratorical skills in part to practices in the care of young children. One speaker in the dialogue lamented the fact that many infants are

> handed over at their birth to some silly little Greek serving-maid, with a male slave, who may be anyone, to help her—quite frequently the most worthless member of the whole establishment, incompetent for any serious service. It is from the foolish tittle-tattle of such persons that the children receive their earliest impressions, while their minds are still green and unformed; and there is not a soul in the whole house who cares a jot what he says or does in the presence of his baby master. (*Dial.* 29)[12]

Tacitus suggested that wet nurses could have negative effects on the child's development. His words underscored the lasting impact of the caregiver on the young child.

Breastfeeding was also associated with a close emotional attachment. The mother's letter cited above suggested that her care for her young son brought some obligation on his part. Favorinus lamented the loss of an emotional connection with the mother when a wet nurse was hired, suggesting the mother would gradually forget her child (*Noct. att.* 12.1.22–23). Although Favorinus's words are not evidence that such mothers were actually less attached to their children, they do suggest the association of an emotional bond with nursing. Similarly, some sources suggest an attachment to nurses that lasted beyond childhood. Many of these bonds were complicated by the slave status of the nurse. Modern readers should not imagine that the affection of a slave toward a free child was uncomplicated.[13] But the sources suggested that such a connection was common.

Women also played a role in the later education of their children. Sometimes they were the one to engage a teacher for the job. In some cases, a famous woman like Cornelia or Julia Procilla was praised for filling in because her husband had died (Plutarch, *Ti. C. Gracc.* 1; Tacitus, *Agr.* 4). But mothers may also have taken up such household tasks as a matter of course. In the second century, Pliny wrote to Corellia Hispulla advising her on the choice of a tutor (*Ep.* 3.3). Nonelite women made similar kinds of decisions. In one letter from Egypt, a woman tells her husband, who is away in military service, "Do not worry about the children: they are well and attend [the lessons of] a woman teacher" (*P.Mich.* 8.464). In such cases women provided for the education of their children.

Yet fathers were also involved in their children's education and were praised for raising children well. For example, Plutarch indicated that the elder Cato undertook the education of his son, though he employed a slave who was a teacher (*Cat. Maj.* 20). Written sources praised fathers for the education of their daughters as well as their sons. Speaking of Gaius's daughter, Laelia, Cicero noted that "it was apparent that her careful usage [of language] was colored by her father's habit" (*Brut.* 211). Another writer criticized fathers who were lavish spenders on other items but neglected to hire good tutors (Ps.-Plutarch, *Lib. ed.* 7).

Some girls were educated alongside boys during the earliest years. In general, children were educated to the extent that the family could afford and considered necessary for the kind of work the child would likely do later in life. Slaves were also educated according to what was expected in their line of work. Few people male or female needed the rhetorical education of a senator. But the many surviving written documents suggest that reading and writing was taught to some degree to a wide segment of the population. Alan Bowman has surmised that many people had literacy skills but fell short of full proficiency.[14] Many people were said "not to know letters": they were unable to sign their names to legal documents. However, such judgments were often made on the ability of a man or woman to write Greek. Some could write letters in their local languages. Still others learned only basic letters and numbers to keep track of supplies and orders.[15]

Education was a sign of the family's social standing, and the education of girls was an opportunity to display one's status. The Latin writer Quintillian gave examples of educated women and suggested that both parents should be as learned as possible (*Inst.* 1.1.6). In a similar vein, Plutarch praised Cornelia, who was "well versed in literature, in playing the lyre, and in geometry, and had been accustomed to listen to philosophical discourses with profit" (*Pomp.* 55). Nevertheless, he also described her as "free from that unpleasant officiousness which such accomplishments are apt to impart to young women." As was the case with Juvenal's satirical description (see chapter 2), Plutarch reflected standard criticism of a woman who was outspoken or appeared more knowledgeable than the men around her. Such comments relied upon the literary education that would have been familiar to his readers. The literary knowledge of elite men and women was a sign of their status. This status was often on display in social settings like the dinner party Juvenal evoked. But the authors also conveyed the risk that women might not acknowledge the status differential of their male peers.

HOUSEHOLD MANAGEMENT AND PRODUCTION

Women were commonly viewed as managers of the household. A first century B.C.E. marriage contract between Apollonia and Philiscus specified that Philiscus would not take another wife or concubine nor "set up another household unless Apollonia is in charge of it" (*P.Tebt* 1.104). The expectation that the wife was "in charge" of the household was widely shared and was attested in literary sources as well. Cicero's sister-in-law, Pomponia, was offended when she was not in charge of a dinner. Cicero quoted her saying to her husband, "I am a guest myself" (*Att.* 5.1.3), suggesting the matron of the house would expect to be responsible for such matters. Cicero referred in numerous letters to his own wife's management of the affairs of his household (e.g., *Fam.* 6, 7, 8, 9, 119, 158, 173).

Household management was a complex affair involving many tasks. Writing in the first century, Columella described the tasks of the female manager (*vilica*) of a large estate. She inspected all the produce and goods brought into the household for quality: grain, wine, tools and utensils, furniture, and clothing. She provided for the storage of food and a system of organization. The vilica cared for the sick within the household, supervised slaves at their work, and saw that everything was clean in the house and barns. She was always instructing others in their tasks or seeking to learn from those with greater knowledge. She had her wool-working ready whenever there was a lull in these other tasks (Columella, *Rust.* 12.1–4). Although Columella presents an idealized picture, the description of her work is also a reminder of the various tasks in large households and underscores that these were imagined as women's work.[16]

Papyri show women of various class levels undertaking these tasks. Letters of women to family members and stewards told of them selling or procuring staples like lentils, oil, wheat, and clothing. For example, an Egyptian woman, Thais, wrote to Tigrios: "If you do come, take out six *artabas* of vegetable-seed and seal them in sacks so that they are ready, and if you can, go up and search out the ass. Sarapodora and Sabinos greet you. Do not sell the young pigs without me. Farewell" (*P. Oxy.* 6.932).[17] Such instructions about everyday matters were common in these letters. In another example, Thermouthias wrote to her mother, "Very many greetings and always good health. I received from Valerius the basket with 20 pairs of wheat cakes and 10 pairs of loaves. Send me the blankets at the current price, and nice wool, 4 fleeces. Give these to Valerius" (*SB* 5.7572).[18] Letters like these show women's management of household resources.

It can be difficult to tell who owns the property mentioned in these letters. Some of these women were managing their own property, and others were managing their husband's affairs. For example, in the letter from Thermouthias, above, she was likely married to Valerius, whom she mentioned in the letter.[19] But the ownership of the items she received or requested was not specified. In many cases it is also difficult to tell the woman's marital status. A letter writer might be widowed, managing property that was hers already along with other property inherited from her husband. Other women were married and managing property that by law belonged to their spouses. The letters make it difficult to discern whose property was involved, in part because women often had a management role with respect to their husband's property.

However, sometimes the records make clear that women were managers of their own property. In the first century B.C.E, one woman posted a memorial inscription to her thirty-six-year-old daughter, "Valeria Maxima, mother, owner of a farm" (CIL 14.3482). Women also left records of their work renting property. In Pompeii, for example, this notice survived: "On the estate of Julia Felix, the daughter of Spurius Felix, the following are for rent: an elegant bath suitable for the best people, shops, rooms above them, and second story apartments, from the Ides of August until the Ides of August five years hence, after which the lease may be renewed by simple agreement" (CIL 4.1136).[20] Another woman collected rent from a tenant on behalf of a different woman (P. Oxy. 33.2680).

Whoever the property belonged to, the tone of these letters indicated that women had authority over the matters they wrote about. Consider this letter, to an unknown addressee: ". . . and sell the wheat necessary and collect the bronze at your house while I come, because I need it. Go to Myrtale and ask her for the money. If she does not want to give it to you, lock her up. See that I do not come and find the wall built up. And make the exedra ready and let the dining room be paved, according to the arrangement Aphys wants; shake out the woolen cloths and the clothes and watch the children and things at home. Watch 'little' Isidora. I pray that you are well" (P.Mil.Vogl. 2.77).[21] The author sent orders about matters of household management. Her relationship to the recipient is unknown, but her tone made it clear that she spoke with authority about matters of this household's financial affairs, repairs or improvements, and oversight of children. She wrote as one who had the power to give instructions about the matters at hand.

Some of the business enterprises women undertook were an extension of their role as household managers. As I discussed in chapter 2, Romans counted commerce and production as "private" concerns, aligning them with an arena that was considered appropriate for women. Furthermore, much of the economic production of the period was centered in the household and therefore came under the woman's domain. A woman's management of business interests would not overstep social boundaries because it was part of her normal sphere of influence. As with other household labor, a woman was sometimes involved in business concerns that were legally owned by her husband, and sometimes she managed her own affairs.

Brickmaking was one area where women owners left evidence of their work. The production of fired bricks increased dramatically with the building projects of the first and second centuries. Some bricks were stamped before firing with the names of the owner (*domini*) and the contractor or production manager (*officinator*), leaving a record of some of the individuals involved. Roughly one third of the domini were women, along with about 6 percent of the officinatores. Some of these women operated brickyards that were formerly owned by their husbands (e.g., Claudia Marcellina, *CIL* 15.934–36; Sergia Paulina, *Bloch* 147).[22] Other women were the only members of their family who produced bricks (e.g., *CIL* 15.1259, 1488).[23] Though a minority, women represented a significant number of the brick producers of these centuries. Classicist Päivi Setälä has argued that the women played the same roles as the men who held these titles.[24]

Women often participated in the local economy, which varied region to region according to the climate and what was produced there. Brick production was an occupation of wealthy landowners, and both men and women took advantage of the opportunity. Sometimes we catch glimpses of similar business ventures by lower-class women. Evidence of women's ownership and registration of camels, for example, occurred in an Egyptian town where camels were an important part of the economy.[25] Graffiti on the wall of a restaurant in Pompeii, one of many establishments where the lower classes of the city would have eaten meals, identified its proprietor as a woman.[26] Women are not found in the evidence as often as men, but they were a regular feature of local economies and they used the wealth and skills they had in much the same ways that men did.

Many women worked in the production of clothing. Within the household, women were in charge of providing clothing for family members and slaves. One legal text discussed the complexities of who owned clothing, given that the ownership of the wool and the slaves involved in production could belong to either husband or wife. The constant assumption in the text was that the wife oversaw the production. The ownership of the clothing hinged on who paid for the wool: for example, "if men's clothes are made on behalf of her husband, they will be his if he paid his wife for the wool" (Pomponius *Dig.* 24.1.31). The assumption was that the wife directed the labor of the slaves in this work, even though the slaves and the wool might belong to either spouse.

Women's participation in the business of the household is also seen in lending and borrowing money. One papyrus from 10 B.C.E. recorded a Jewish woman's repayment of a debt (*CPJ* 148). Other documents showed loans between women (*P.Kron* 17; *P.Tebt.* 2.389; *CIL* 4.8203). Lending money was one important element of patron-client relationships (see chapter 5), so these documents are evidence that women participated in those roles. The pursuit of honor through the cultivation of patron and client relationships was one way to enhance the economic and social well-being of the household and thus a natural part of the work both men and women were engaged in. But there was also an economic function to the loans. Women lent or borrowed money to further their economic interests.

Women's management of the household also included their ownership and management of slaves. One papyrus from Egypt recorded a woman, Segathis, apprenticing her slave girl,

Taorsenouphis, to a weaver (*Stud.Pal.* 22.40). Another woman petitioned the local ruler because of an injury to her slave, Peina (*P.Oxy.* 50.3555). In another legal document, Philotera leased her slave Zosime to her son as a wet nurse for another slave child. Sillis paid a salary to Philotera for the use of her slave, and Philotera agreed to safeguard the child and the wet nurse (*BGU* 4.1058). Transactions like these were an expected part of everyday life, and they show the participation of women in slave ownership and management.

In wealthy households, slave women also served managerial functions. The role of the vilica in managing a country estate has already been noted above. The vilica was a slave woman whose "duties were extensive, stretching from the overall maintenance of the villa, the organization of provisions and cooked meals for the slave *familia*, the general care and guardianship of the laborers, to the supervision of a whole range of domestic and industrial activities carried out at the farmstead."[27] On a large farm, a host of other slaves, both male and female, carried out these tasks under the supervision of the vilica.

Male slaves often filled other clerical and administrative functions within the household, an indication of their relatively high status compared to females. Although most of the titles referring to the financial administration of the household applied to men, a few inscriptions assigned titles like *a manu* or *librariae* to women (e.g., *CIL* 6.9523, 9525, 37802). These women might have been secretaries or clerks who kept track of the goods that came in and out of the family's storeroom.

Slave women performed a wide variety of tasks within the wealthy Roman household. Many households had only a few slaves, who likely performed many tasks. Wealthier households could assign slaves to specialized tasks, and the ability to do so became a status marker.[28] Although from an earlier period, Plautus gave a glimpse into the attendant of a wealthy matron. Speaking of a lover's attempts to gain access to such a woman, Plautus wrote: "He's granted a night: the whole establishment is hired, the dress-folder, the masseur, the guardian of jewelry, the fan-bearers, the sandal-carriers, the female singers, the maids with treasure boxes, the ones who bring messages and the ones who bring messages back, the thieves of bread and sustenance. While the lover is being generous to them, he himself becomes destitute" (*Trin.* 250–255). Plautus's list included a number of specialized slaves. Belonging to such a family was also a marker of relative status for slaves, who recorded their job titles in inscriptions.

Many women slaves served as the personal servants of women. Some were hairdressers (*ornatrices*), employed to create the elaborate hairstyles that became popular in the first century (see figure 3.1). Others, *vestiplicae*, cared for clothes (e.g., *CIL* 6.33393, 37825). *Pedisequae* were slaves who followed the matron on foot when she went out or ran errands on her behalf (e.g., *CIL* 6.6335, 9266, 9775). Susan Treggiari has argued that job specialization contributed to the morale among the household slaves and allowed the system to function more smoothly.[29]

OTHER OCCUPATIONS

Some jobs were extensions of household production. For example, in the first century as cloth came to be produced more widely outside of the household, women worked in its production. The walls of a factory in Pompeii listed many women employed there as spinners. Similarly, one papyrus recorded female textile workers of a production facility (*BGU* 10.1942). On a smaller scale, a letter from Apollonia described her actions in producing or contracting to produce thread for clothing (*P.Oxy.* 31.2593).[30] Inscriptions often simply stated a woman's occupation: for example, as clothes makers (*CIL* 6.33920), menders (*CIL* 6.9884), and wool weighers (*CIL* 6.9496).[31] Many men also worked in the production of clothing, especially as weavers, but in other tasks as well.

The occupations of women that were mentioned in inscriptions covered a wide variety of fields. Women were mosaic workers (*CIL* 5.7044) and perfumers (*CIL* 6.1006), jewelers (*CIL* 6.5972, 9435), and makers of fine clothing (*CIL* 6.9213, 9214). Women worked in the production of a variety of goods.

Women also sold goods in the marketplaces. Figure 6.1 offers a visual image of a woman merchant. Numerous women undertook similar work as sellers of bottles (*CIL* 6.9488), fruit (*CIL* 6.37819), grain (*CIL* 6.9683, 9684), salt (*IG* 2.11244), fish (*CIL* 6.9801), incense (*CIL* 6.9934), and cloth (*CIL* 2.4318a).

Jewish women likely worked in similar ways. There are few explicit references to Jewish women in sources of this period, making it difficult to find explicit evidence of their tasks. Miriam Peskowitz has chronicled evidence for Jewish women performing similar kinds of jobs found in later (Tannaitic) sources.[32] Given these similarities, it seems likely that Jewish women worked at the same sorts of tasks as their Greek and Roman counterparts.

Women were also entertainers of various kinds. Inscriptions recorded women singers (*CIL* 6.10132 [*ILS* 5231]; *ILS* 9347), actors (*CIL* 6.10127 [*ILS* 5262]), and musicians (*IG* 2.11496; *CIL* 6.10125 [*ILS* 5244]). For example, in 86 B.C.E., the city of Delphi honored Polynota, a harpist from Thebes who performed at the Pythian games. They gave her a crown and 500 drachmas, and posted an inscription:

> to commend Polygnota . . . for her piety and reverence towards
> the god and for her dedication to her profession; to bestow on

FIGURE 6.1 Marketplace sign. Archaeological Museum Ostia. Photo: Gianni Dagli Orit/The Art Archive at Art Resource, NY. Used by permission.

her and on her descendants the guest-friendship of the city, the right to consult the oracle, the privileges of being heard first, of safety, of exemption from taxes, and of front seating at the games held by the city, the right of owning land and a house and all the other honors ordinarily awarded to other benefactors of the city; to invite her to the town hall to the public hearth, and provide her with a victim to sacrifice to Apollo. (*Pleket* 6.G)[33]

Women were gladiators and athletes who competed in games (*CIG* 6855.G).[34] Wealthy women were also patrons of these forms of entertainment. They paid the gladiators or actors, or built the theaters in which they performed (see chapter 5).

Women also worked as doctors and midwives. Some women in these positions were slaves, and others were free or freedpersons. One funerary inscription identified "Antonia Thallusa, freedwoman of the emperor, a midwife" (*CIL* 6.8947).[35] The second-century medical writer Soranus discussed the qualifications and training of midwives (*Gynecology* 1). Other inscriptions and papyri mentioned women who were physicians or healers.[36]

Although it runs contrary to modern expectations, some women also worked as teachers. A papyrus letter, cited above regarding elements of household management, stated that the children attended classes with a woman teacher (*P.Mich.* 8.464). Figure 6.2 shows a mummy portrait that identifies the deceased woman, Hermione, as a *grammatikē* or teacher of grammar and literature. Women were less likely than men to be educated in this period, and so fewer women were qualified to work as teachers. However, the sources show no surprise at the presence of women in these roles, suggesting there was nothing prohibiting their activity.

NEW TESTAMENT OCCUPATIONS

Like many of the women whose names appear in literary texts and inscriptions, the occupations of New Testament women are

FIGURE 6.2 Hermione Grammatike. Girton College Library. © The Mistress and Fellows, Girton College, Cambridge. Used by permission.

often unknown. The Samaritan woman (John 4:4–42), the women who provided for Jesus (Luke 8:1–3), Nympha (Col 4:15), Euodia and Syntyche (Phil 4:2), and Phoebe (Rom 16:1) are examples of women whose occupations were not mentioned.

In a few places, however, there are glimpses of the jobs women did. Tabitha's production of clothing (Acts 9:39) situated her as a participant in this traditional female task. The description of her as "devoted to good works and to charity" may suggest the clothing was made to give to others. Acts does not state what kind of occupation allowed Tabitha to fund these projects. But in that cultural context, readers would likely have assumed that Tabitha both initiated this work and provided the funds necessary to complete it.

Acts also mentioned Paul's associate Prisca, along with Paul and Aquila, as a tentmaker by occupation (Acts 18:3). Again, few details are provided. Against the cultural background of the time, readers might well imagine that Prisca and Aquila worked together in their business as they traveled from place to place, and that Prisca contributed as much to the household economy as she did to the spread of the gospel (cf. Romans 16:3; Acts 18:26).

More explicitly, Acts recorded Lydia's occupation as a "dealer in purple cloth" (Acts 16:14). The details of Lydia's business were not described, nor was the reason that brought her from her hometown of Thyatira to residence in Philippi, where she had a home. The phrase "when she and her household were baptized" (Acts 16:15), suggests Lydia was the head of a household with slaves and children or other family members. Presumably Lydia's business interests supported her household and allowed her to offer hospitality to a visiting teacher like Paul.

Elsewhere in the New Testament, we see the expectation that women contributed to their household economy as managers of the household. The qualifications for male and female deacons included good management of their children and households (1 Tim 3:11–12). Similarly, widows were women who had cultivated the virtues associated with household tasks like raising children and showing hospitality. The use of these tasks as qualifications for church office was a reminder that management of the household often signified virtue and was a way that women could gain status in their communities. Thus, women's work in the household was not simply restrictive in the way that modern readers may imagine it. Instead, these tasks gave women authority over segments of social, economic, and religious life.

Chapter 7

Speech and Silence

IN LIGHT OF THE PREVIOUS CHAPTERS, it may come as no surprise that women's speech was also a regular part of life in the New Testament period. Women spoke in the course of their occupations, whatever they were. Wealthier women directed their business dealings and commanded slaves. They interacted with patrons or clients. Women of various classes spoke in the course of directing other members of their households, teaching, and pursuing their social and political interests.

Women did not enter into acts of speech as the equals of men. In principle, society viewed women as inferior to men. They were expected to show their deference to men of higher rank, and this could be expressed through silence. Political speeches and rhetoric were a male domain.

However, the silence of women was not an absolute rule that applied uniformly in every situation. As I discussed in chapter 2, culture does not simply give its members rules to live by, as if the rules were one size fits all and applied uniformly to every situation. Instead, culture also supplies the social understanding required to apply the rules. Consider this example of modern rules for speech: American culture values freedom of expression, but if someone proclaims his or her political allegiances loudly in the middle of a movie, that individual will likely be thrown out of the theater. The cultural "rule" of free speech does not govern every situation. People within the culture do not usually experience silence in the movie theater as a contradiction of the rule of free speech. Culture provides the social understanding that shapes our speech and silence in particular situations. The same person may be silent in one place and speak forcefully in a different context, and in each case he or she may be operating well within the expected social norms.

Furthermore, conventions of speech and silence were complex and sometimes in tension. Ancient Mediterranean cultures described both silence and bold speech as virtues. In some cases, authors presented silence as evidence of self-control and speech as self-indulgence. However, in other situations, bold speech was praised as evidence of bravery whereas silence showed weakness and cowardice. Culturally, speech and silence could mean different things, depending on the circumstances.

Women could be praised or criticized for both speech and silence, just as men could. Because social norms suggested silence indicated deference to one's superiors, women's silence sometimes appeared as socially expected passivity. However, in other cases a woman's silence could be interpreted as active, virtuous behavior. While women could be criticized for speaking too much in the wrong context, other social norms encouraged women to speak and upheld examples of those whose speech showed wisdom and courage.

I begin below with a discussion of some expressions of the "rules" of silence from the culture at large. Certain writings support the impression that the rules of ancient culture silenced women completely. However, even in these sources we see some of the conventions that supported women's speech as well. The chapter surveys a wider array of evidence for women's speech and silence before returning to the New Testament.

CULTURAL NORMS OF SILENCE

Historians have often turned to Livy's history of the repeal of the Oppian Laws as an example of the limitations on women's speech. Livy wrote in the early Imperial period about events that took place in 195 B.C.E. Two senators sought to dismantle an earlier set of measures that restricted elaborate displays of wealth.

In particular, the earlier laws forbade multicolored clothing or travel in a carriage around Rome and limited how much gold a woman could wear. According to Livy, a large number of women turned out in favor of the repeal of these laws, advocating in the streets around the forum as the senators made their way there. The respected orator, Cato, spoke against the repeal. He cited the women's behavior as part of his argument: "What sort of practice is this, of running out into the streets and blocking the roads and speaking to other women's husbands? Could you not have made the same requests, each of your own husband, at home? Or are you more attractive outside and to other women's husbands than your own? And yet, not even at home, if modesty would keep matrons within the limits of their proper rights, did it become you to concern yourselves with the question of what laws should be adopted in this place or repealed" (*Hist.* 34.2.8–11).[1] Cato went on to portray the women's speech as disorderly behavior that would only increase if the senators repealed the Oppian Laws. Modern interpreters have often cited Cato's words as evidence that women were not allowed to speak outside of the home or to address political matters.

However, the larger context of Cato's speech contradicted this conclusion. The quote above was prefaced by these words: "Had not respect for the dignity and modesty of some individuals among [the women] rather than of the sex as a whole kept me silent, lest they should seem to have been rebuked by a consul, I should have said, 'What sort of practice is this?'" (*Hist.* 34.2.8). Cato quoted what he might have said to the women but did not. His words were not spoken directly to the women in order to limit their speech. They were directed at his colleagues in the senate in an attempt to persuade them. Cato's criticism of the women's speech should be read in its context as part of an argument in favor of retaining the Oppian laws. His words are evidence that norms of silence could be evoked to persuade others. They are not evidence that women were forbidden to speak.

To the contrary, Cato's words suggest that a woman's ability to speak without censure was dependent on her social status. Cato quoted what he would have liked to have said to the women. But he noted that "the dignity and modesty of some" of the women prevented him from saying these things. Some of the protesters were high-ranking women, and Cato deemed it inappropriate to rebuke them openly, even though he disapproved of their actions.

Furthermore, Cato's opponent, Valerius, affirmed instances where the speech of women was a good thing. Valerius pointed out that it was conventional for women to speak in situations of political need. "What new thing have the matrons done in coming out into the streets in crowds in a case that concerned them?" (*Hist.* 34.5.7). He cited matrons who mediated between men in times of war and women who contributed wealth to the treasury in times of civic need (34.5.8–10). Through these examples, Valerius reminded his listeners that women's speech was not unusual. Indeed, it could be praised and upheld as an exemplar of bravery and civic-mindedness.

Valerius also noted that Cato himself had praised women's speech. He pointed out that Cato had collected and written down the stories he told: "Let me unroll your own *Origines* against you" (*Hist.* 34.5.8). (*Origines* was a work by Cato that now exists only in fragments.) By noting that Cato had praised women's speech in some circumstances, Valerius undercut Cato's assertion that women should never speak on political matters. Valerius's stories of women brought to mind familiar history in which women's speech was expected and even praiseworthy.

Valerius expected that women, like men, would speak to situations that affected them directly. "But what no one wonders that all, men and women alike, have done in matters that concern them, do we wonder that the women have done in a case peculiarly their own? What now have they done? We have proud ears, upon my word, if, although masters do not scorn to hear the petitions of slaves, we complain that we are appealed to by respectable women" (*Hist.* 34.5.12–13). Valerius's words upheld the common hierarchical distinction between men and women, just as Cato's did. His comparison with a slave speaking to his master underscored the imbalance of power between men and women.

Yet his point was that if even slaves were allowed to petition masters, how much more so should distinguished women speak regarding matters that concerned them. He drew on cultural norms that gave lower-status people reasons to speak.

The successful repeal of the Oppian Laws suggests that the women's speech was not entirely outside the boundaries of expected behavior. If Cato's words were an accurate description of the rules of social interaction, we might expect a different outcome. But in this case, their speech was persuasive. Livy wrote: "When these speeches against and for the bill had been delivered, the next day an even greater crowd of women appeared in public, and all of them in a body beset the doors of the Bruti, who were vetoing their colleagues' proposal, and they did not desist until the threat of veto was withdrawn by the tribunes. After that there was no question that all the tribes would vote to repeal the law" (*Hist.* 34.8.1–2). The women's persistence was ultimately effective in achieving their goals. Livy's description did not convey disapproval of their success.

This analysis of Livy's writing suggests that it was possible to evoke women's silence as a rule of culture, but that the rule did not apply in the same way in every situation. The speech of women could be praised when exercised to protect their cities. Women's speech was also expected in matters that concerned them. While the realm of their concern would certainly apply to matters of household management and social influence, in this instance it also included political advocacy. The importance of social status was also visible in Cato's restraint in speaking to them. A woman's qualification to speak even to senators was shaped by her social standing.

Other literary sources that stated norms of women's silence conveyed a similar tension. Many scholars have cited Juvenal's criticism of a woman's speech at a dinner party, which I quoted in part in chapter 2:

> But she's much worse, the woman who as soon as she's taken her place at dinner is praising Virgil and forgiving Elissa on her

deathbed, who pits the poets against one another and assesses them. . . . The schoolteachers give way, the teachers of rhetoric are beaten, the whole party falls silent, there'll not be a word from any lawyer or auctioneer—and not even from another woman. . . . Don't let the lady reclining next to you have her own rhetorical style or brandish phrases before hurling her rounded syllogism at you. Don't let her know the whole of history. Let there be a few things in books that she doesn't even understand. I loathe the woman who is forever referring to Palaemon's *Grammar* and thumbing through it, observing all the laws and rules of speech, or who quotes lines I've never heard, a female scholar. . . . Husbands should be allowed their grammatical oddities. (Juvenal, *Sat.* 6.434–447)[2]

Juvenal's satirical remarks made sense in a cultural context in which wealthy women were educated and capable of speaking on subjects like literature, history, and grammar. Furthermore, these women reclined alongside their husbands at dinner parties where such topics were discussed. If Juvenal's criticism hit home for his readers, it was because they saw this woman upstaging her male peers, to whom, according to social custom, she should defer. Juvenal would not have criticized the same woman speaking on different subjects, or speaking on the same subjects to a lower-class person, child, or slave. The interplay of speech and status made it possible that he could criticize her speech before her male peers.

Plutarch's writings conveyed support of both silence and speech. He also indicated that women should defer to their husbands in speech. "A wife should speak only to her husband or through her husband, and should not feel aggrieved if, like a piper, she makes nobler music through another's tongue" (*Conj. praec.* 32).[3] Yet Plutarch elsewhere quoted women speakers with approval. For example, he wrote of Olympias "who, when a young courtier married a beautiful woman with a bad reputation, observed, 'He has no sense, or he would not have married with his eyes'" (*Conj. praec.* 24). Plutarch then affirmed the same point, that one ought not marry on the basis of appearance. Plutarch quoted the words of women five more times in the course of this work (*Conj. praec.* 18, 31, 40, 46, 48). His adages about women's silence appeared alongside their words, which were quoted with approval.

Thus, even these statements of the "rule" of women's silence conveyed knowledge and affirmation of conventions of women's speech. If modern readers assume that women's speech was not always forbidden, then we may return to the ancient sources with a new set of questions. As we explore women's speech, we should be interested not only in statements of the rules but also in evidence of the social understanding people used to live by the rules of culture.

EVIDENCE FOR THE SPEECH AND SILENCE OF WOMEN

In the pages that follow, I present additional evidence for the cultural norms regarding women's silence and speech. I look at examples from four kinds of sources: philosophy, fiction, inscriptions, and letters. None of these sources gives direct evidence of the speech of actual women. They are all highly stylized in various ways. However, we do get a sense of what both author and reader took for granted about women's speech or silence, and in such moments, we glimpse some of the social understanding that shaped the application of the rules of culture.

Viewed in their literary context, the speech or silence of women can give us additional information about the social norms of the time. I approach the evidence asking questions such as, What were the purposes of women's silence? To whom did women speak? Where did they speak? What subjects did they speak about? In what situations does their silence occur? Framing the exploration this way helps me to avoid assumptions about the nature of women's speech as public or private (see chapter 2). It also allows me to look for speech that is unremarkable as well as speech that provokes praise or blame.

Silence as a Virtue

The idea that women could be criticized for speaking reflects the social context in which women were perceived to be of lower status than men. Silence was expected as a sign of deference to those of higher rank. Younger people were to defer to their elders, slaves to masters, and women to men.[4] For example, one story from Plutarch's *Lives* identified silence as a sign of the high standing of the other person present. Following the assassination of Caesar, the people listened to a discourse by Brutus "without either expressing resentment at what had been done or appearing to approve of it; they showed, however, by their deep silence, that while they pitied Caesar, they respected Brutus" (Plutarch *Caes.* 66).[5] The people showed deference to Brutus through their silence. In the same way, the expectation of women's silence in the sources above reflects their status differential.

However, silence was not only a sign of deference but could be a virtue as well. This was true for men as well as women. An example of silence among men as evidence of virtue occurred in Apuleius's story *Metamorphoses*, or *The Golden Ass*. The narrator and traveler, Lucian, who was later magically transformed into a donkey, encountered a wealthy aunt in the town he was visiting. Although her attendant recognized Lucian, he was afraid to speak to his aunt because she was a woman of high standing: "'I am embarrassed in front of a woman whom I do not know,' I answered, suddenly blushing, and I just stood there looking at the ground. Then she turned and stared at me. 'He inherited that well-bred behavior,' she said, 'from his pure and virtuous mother, Salvia'" (*Metam.* 2.2).[6] Here, Lucian's reluctance to speak to a woman who is clearly his social superior was praised as good manners. Their family ties gave him an opportunity to speak, but her high standing made it plausible that he would not. His aunt intervened, addressing him first, and offered her assistance and patronage. This fictional work assumed readers would understand the propriety of Lucian's silence in the presence of his high-ranking aunt.

In some instances, silence was also portrayed as evidence of philosophical achievement. Plutarch called it "the mark of a man who is making progress" not to tell others of his achievements. Instead, he would "keep all this to himself and put the seal of silence on it." Although training in oratory was the pinnacle of the educational system, Plutarch argued that the philosopher who advanced beyond oratory adopted "another bearing of silence and amazement" (*Virt. prof.* 10).

The virtue of self-control also informed Plutarch's stories depicting silence as bravery. The women of Melos conspired with their male relatives against the Carians, who planned to kill them after a banquet. The women brought concealed weapons into the banquet, and at a designated time the men seized the weapons and slew their opponents. Plutarch concluded with the comment, "It is right and proper to admire both the silence and the courage of the women, and that not a single one of them among so many was led by timidity to turn coward even voluntarily" (*Mulier. virt*).[7] In this case, silence was evidence of self-control exercised under difficult circumstances. Another example was that of a woman named Micca, who endured a beating from a tyrant rather than submit to him: "She bravely bore the painful blows in silence" (*Mulier. virt*). Similar stories were told of men as well, who, when confronted with a tyrannical ruler, showed their superior virtue through silence (e.g., Plutarch, *Cam.* 22).

Thus, silence was not simply viewed as mere passivity. Although silence could be criticized as weakness in some circumstances, in other cases it was viewed as appropriate deference, and in still others it was an act of courage. Controlling the tongue was evidence of the virtue of self-control, something that was difficult to maintain when in danger or under threat. In such instances, silence could be a virtue rather than a weakness.

Speech on Political Subjects

Stories and histories represented a number of women as speakers on political topics. One notable example is Appian's recounting of a tax imposed on women in the civil war period prior to Augustus's reign. The triumvirs—Octavian, Antony, and Lepidus—imposed a tax on the 1,400 richest women in Rome. The women protested. They first visited three women related to these men: Octavius's sister, Antony's mother, and Antony's wife, Fulvia. The first two women received their request, but Fulvia rejected them. The women then made their way to the triumvirs in the forum, where one of the women, Hortensia, spoke in protest. Appian quoted her speech at some length (*Bell. civ.* 4.32–33). The triumvirs were angry that the women opposed the tax and also that a woman made a political speech while the men were silent. "They ordered the lictors to drive them away from the tribunal, which they proceeded to do until cries were raised by the multitude outside, when the lictors desisted and the triumvirs said they would postpone till the next day the consideration of the matter" (4.34).[8] The next day they reduced the number of women taxed to four hundred and added a tax on a wider group of male citizens.

Plutarch's parallel *Lives* also included a number of women whose speech was quoted at key moments in history.[9] One example, Chilonis, was the daughter of King Leonidas of Sparta. She was married to Cleombrotus, who had become an enemy of the king. Cleombrotus fled to the sanctuary of Poseidon, and Chilonis, although she had supported her father in the political turmoil, joined her husband there. When Leonidas confronted Chilonis's husband, he sat, silent and at a loss (Plutarch, *Ag. Cleom.* 17). But Chilonis addressed her father. She began by pointing to the difficult situation that both her husband and father brought about for her. Although she had sided with her father against her husband, she now faced further difficulty if her father would not heed her words and spare her husband. She argued that killing Cleombrotus would confirm people's fears about the power her father held, because it would show "that royal power is a thing so great and so worth fighting for that for its sake it is right to slay a son-in-law and ignore a child" (*Ag. Cleom.* 17). Chilonis spoke as a suppliant of her father on a political subject. Plutarch also mentioned the crowd standing with them: they were moved by her goodness and devotion. Her words convinced her father to spare Cleombrotus's life and send him into exile. Chilonis chose to remain with her father.

Plutarch's stories continued in a similar vein of politically engaged speech. One of the most ancient tales, told and retold by Romans, was the story of Rome's founding. Although Sabine women had been forcefully taken by Rome, the women intervened to stop a war between the two clans. Plutarch's version of the peace process quoted a Sabine woman, Hersilia, at length (*Rom.* 19.4–7). Other women in Plutarch's stories took on similar roles as political emissaries. One Roman woman, Volumnia, convinced her son not to attack the city (*Cor.* 33–36). Octavia forged an alliance between her husband, Mark Antony, and her brother, Octavian, and orchestrated an exchange of military forces (*Ant.* 35.3–5).

In another kind of political speech, women characters spurred men on to acts of political bravery and sacrifice. One example was Porcia, the wife of Brutus (Plutarch, *Brut.* 13.6–10). As the plot built toward the assassination of Julius Caesar, Porcia had noticed Brutus's unease. She did not question him about his secrets until first putting herself to a test. She cut her own arm quite badly without letting others know. She then spoke to Brutus, declaring herself to be his partner even in pain.

> "I know that woman's nature is thought too weak to endure a secret; but good rearing and excellent companionship go far towards strengthening the character, and it is my happy lot to be both the daughter of Cato and the wife of Brutus. Before this I put less confidence in these advantages, but now I know that I am superior even to pain." Thus having spoken, she showed him her wound and explained her test; whereupon Brutus, amazed, and lifting his hands to heaven, prayed that he might succeed in his undertaking and thus show himself a worthy husband of Porcia. (*Brut.* 13)

Porcia drew on her social standing and her self-testing to present herself as a worthy confidant. Brutus interpreted her words and actions as a catalyst for his own.[10]

Jewish works also portrayed women who spoke on political subjects. In the apocryphal story of Judith, the heroine called together the elders of her town and spoke to them at some length (Jud 8:11–27). She declared that she had a plan to save them from their enemies (8:32–34), prayed and prepared herself (Jud 9:1–14), and carried out her plot against Holofernes the Assyrian. Judith spoke to Holofernes several times before she killed him, and her story concluded with her song of praise (Jud 16:1–17).

The Greek novels of the first and second centuries reinforced the propriety of women's speech on political matters. For example, in the story *Chaereas and Callirhoe*, Callirhoe spoke directly to her husband, Chaereas, regarding political matters. He was a military victor who conquered the Persians who had held Callirhoe captive. After they were reunited, Callirhoe directed Chaereas to return the Queen of Persia to her place with the king. Chaereas had intended to keep the queen as a slave for Callirhoe, but he changed his mind in accordance with her wishes.

Women also appeared in more formal court and assembly proceedings in these stories. These settings privileged the voices of male characters. One of the twists in Callirhoe's story happened when her second husband, Dionysius, accused another man of having intentions toward his wife after that man delivered a letter to her that was really from Chaereas, her first husband. The courtroom scene was an affair between men, and in the initial hearing Callirhoe was not present. The king and the male opponents spoke. However, Callirhoe was present for the final judgment in the courtroom scene, and she cried out when she saw Chaereas, whom she thought was dead: "Chaereas, are you alive?" (*Chaer.* 5.8). Her recognition and statement caused the mystery around the case to unwind, and the case dissolved.[11]

Callirhoe's story also included an appearance in the assembly. At the end of their story Chaereas and Callirhoe returned home to a warm greeting. Chaereas told their tale to a packed assembly.

Those who rushed to hear Chaereas's tale included both men and women. "More quickly than words can tell the theater was filled with men and women. When Chaereas came in by himself, they all cried out, men as well as women, 'Call Callihroe in!'" (*Chaer.* 8.7) Men and women then joined in praising the couple. After Chaereas's speech, there was a vote to confer citizenship on those who assisted the couple. Although it seems appropriate to assume that only male citizens participated in the vote, there was no indication that the women left the assembly.

The trial proceedings in *Leukippe and Cleitophon* were likewise dominated by the speeches of men. Thersandros, who brought the charges, considered Leukippe his slave, which made her speech less likely. Instead, she acted to defend herself by undergoing a test of her virginity to prove her version of the story was true. Upon her entrance into a cave, the god Pan produced beautiful music, which was taken as a sign of her virginity (*Leuc. Clit.* 8.13–14). However, after Leukippe's status was established in this way, she then spoke at a formal dinner gathering and narrated her story (8.15).

Jewish and Christian stories also included courtroom scenes where women spoke. In the apocryphal book, Susanna, the main character was falsely accused of adultery. Susanna did not defend herself in court, but she did cry out with a loud voice after being sentenced: "O eternal God, you know what is secret and are aware of all things before they come to be; you know that these men have given false evidence against me. And now I am to die, though I have done none of the wicked things that they have charged against me!" (Sus 42). Her cry caused Daniel to speak up and initiate further investigation, resulting in her vindication.

Similarly, a second-century Christian story, the *Acts of Paul and Thecla*, included court scenes where women were present and spoke. Thecla was a young woman whose devotion to Paul's message got her in trouble with authorities. In the first instance, she was brought before the governor to judgment. Thecla did not speak, but her mother, a local elite woman named Theocleia, spoke up demanding her daughter's execution (*ATh* 20). Thecla was miraculously saved by God's intervention (*ATh* 22) but later underwent a similar trial. In that case, when the governor condemned her to the beasts, "the women there were astonished and cried out before the judgment seat, 'A wicked judgment! An unholy judgment!'" (*ATh* 27). A wealthy woman, Tryphaena, was also present in the court and took Thecla under her protection until the games began. After she was again saved by divine intervention, Thecla made a formal statement of her identity and faith before the governor (*ATh* 37).

Letters and inscriptions offer another kind of evidence that may be helpful in considering the speech of women. As I noted in chapter 5, there are many examples of inscriptions recording civic benefactions of women.[12] Consider this example from first century Cartima in Roman Spain:

> Junia Rustica, daughter of Decimus, first and perpetual priestess in the *municipium* of Cartima, restored the public porticos that had decayed due to old age, gave land for a bathhouse, reimbursed the public taxes, set up a bronze statue of Mars in the forum, gave at her own cost porticos next to the bathhouse on her own land, with a pool and a statue of Cupid, and dedicated them after giving a feast and public shows. Having remitted the expense, she made and dedicated the statues that were decreed by the council of Cartima for herself and her son, Gaius Fabius Junianus, and she likewise made and dedicated at her own cost the statue for Gaius Fabius Fabianus, her husband. (*CIL* 2.1956)[13]

Like many women of her era, Junia Rustica was a wealthy woman and an important benefactor of her city.

Although the inscription does not represent an actual speech by a woman in the civic space, it can still give us some insight into the social expectations regarding speech. The language represented the process by which many such inscriptions were established, as Emily Hemelrijk wrote: "Her priesthood and civic munificence led to a polite exchange between her and the local council, which, in gratitude for her benefactions, decreed public statues for herself and her son. Accepting the honor, she remitted the expense, setting up the statues herself."[14] Hemelrijk argued that Junia likely had input into and perhaps even drafted the wording of the inscription. Although some inscriptions were worded on behalf of the assembly to the honoree (that is, in the dative case: "*to* Junia Rustica . . ."), this text is in the nominative case, as if Junia wrote on her own behalf.[15]

Such inscriptions were part of the self-representations of the elite and sub-elite classes of this period, who sought honor through the pursuit of civic offices and donations (see chapter 5). While not direct evidence of women's speech, they suggest that it was possible and even desirable in some circumstances to portray a woman's voice in this context. There is no apparent hesitancy to represent a woman patron in this way.

Persuasion and Advocacy

Women often spoke in order to pursue the interests of family members. Women characters in the Greek novels appealed to family members and authority figures, both successfully and unsuccessfully. Chaereas's parents each pleaded with him from the harbor not to sail off in search of Callirhoe (*Chaer.* 5.5). The narrative recorded short speeches by both his mother and his father. Neither persuaded Chaereas to stay.

Women also spoke on their own behalf. The women characters in the fictional stories spoke in a variety of settings to people with authority. Sometimes this authority was due to political position, and other times it was simply the circumstances of the events. For example, in *An Ephesian Tale*, Anthia persuaded a goatherd not to rape her (*Eph.* 2.9). She drew on her former social status as a matron who had been taken prisoner. She later spoke without success to pirates, whom she wanted to leave her alone to die. However, she did convince Psammis, to whom she was then sold, that she was dedicated to Isis as a virgin and should be left alone until she was of age (3.11).

The sources did not always represent women as telling the truth. In the Greek novels, both men and women lied to achieve their aims. Melite, a character in *Leukippe and Cleitophon*, deceived her husband about the nature of her relationship with Kleitophon (*Leuc. Clit.* 6.9–10). Some lies had positive aims, however, like Anthia's claim that she was dedicated to Isis. Similarly, Callirhoe deceived Dionysius that he was the father of her child so that the child would grow up a free and well-born person (*Chaer.* 3.1–2). These characters drew on a variety of tactics to persuade others.

Characters also communicated by letter when separated by distance. Both Chaereas and Callirhoe sent letters, the texts of which were quoted in the narrative. Having been reunited with Chaereas, Callirhoe wrote to Dionysius, the man who had bought her as a slave but made her his wife. She instructed him regarding their son: "I entrust him to you to bring up and educate in a way worthy of us. Do not let him learn what a stepmother is like. You have a daughter as well as a son; two children are enough for you. Marry them to each other when he comes of age; and send him to Syracuse so that he can see his grandfather too" (*Chaer.* 8.4). Like many of the papyrus letters that I discuss below, Callirhoe's fictional letter represented her voice and wishes. The wording was kind but also clearly stated her expectations.

Evidence in the papyrus documents supports the practice of letter writing seen in the fictional accounts. These letters also represented women's voices on matters of personal interest. The language of letters to family was not highly stylized and may have represented some of the ways women spoke. One woman wrote a letter of condolence: "Be of good courage. I was as grieved and I wept over the fortunate one as I wept over Didymas, and I did everything that was fitting, and (so did) all of my people. . . . But all the same one can do nothing in the face of such things. Therefore comfort one another" (*P.Oxy.* 1.115).[16] Another woman wrote to ensure that a relative would take advantage of an official's visit to secure an unspecified privilege for a boy in the family: "Come quickly before the prefect, so we can have the boy examined." She also reported actions with regard to the family's landholdings: "The southern basin of the 17 (arouras) has been sold for the cattle. Your cattle ate one aroura and went to Pansoue. . . . The west of the vegetable field was released for hay cutting" (*BL* 1.167).[17] Another woman inquired about a parent: "And how is my father? Please, send me news because he was ill when he left me" (*SB* 5.7572).[18] (Also see the letters cited in chapter 6.) Women "spoke" in these letters about matters of family concern. But their interests were not only personal, as in the loss of a family member, but also pertained to the family's business interests and social standing.

Prayer and Prophecy

Many ancient sources represented women praying aloud, both alone and with others, on topics both personal and corporate. Women did not appear as frequently as men in these speaking roles, but their prayers were often similarly worded. The sources included women from different religious backgrounds and circumstances.

Jewish women often appeared in literary sources, lifting their voices in prayer.[19] The fictional work *Joseph and Aseneth* represented Aseneth in prayer numerous times. Her prayers, quoted at considerable length, focused on confession of sin and petition for spiritual rescue (e.g., *JosAs* 12–13, 21.10–21). In 3 Maccabees, women joined with men to pray in the temple at a time of national crisis (e.g., 3 Macc 1:16–29; 5:48–51). Pseudo-Philo retold stories from scripture, and he often included or expanded the prayers of women characters like Jael (*Bib. Ant.* 31.5–6), Deborah (32.1–17) and Seila (Jephtha's daughter, 40.5–7).

Hannah's prayers in Pseudo-Philo included explicit reflection upon whether the prayers were spoken out loud. The narrator retold the story of Hannah's desire for a child in 1 Sam 1. He restated Hannah's prayer of 1 Sam 1:11 in this way: "Did you not, Lord, search out the heart of all generations before you formed the world? Now what womb is born opened or dies closed unless you wish it? And now let my prayer ascend before you today lest I go down from here empty, because you know my heart, how I have walked before you from the day of my youth" (*Bib. Ant.* 50.4).[20] Pseudo-Philo followed the description in the biblical narrative that Hannah prayed silently. "Hannah did not want to pray out loud as all people do because she thought, 'Perhaps I am not worthy to be heard'" (*Bib. Ant.* 50.5). This comment suggested that praying aloud was conventional; it gave a reason that Hannah was not doing so when the priest Eli saw her and assumed she was disturbed. Following the birth of Samuel, Hannah again prayed aloud (1 Sam 2:1–10; expanded in *(Bib. Ant.* 51.3–6). Her prayer included the affirmation: "Speak, speak, Hannah, and do not be silent" (*Bib. Ant.* 51.6).

Women characters in the Greek novels also prayed aloud as they thanked the gods or appealed to them for assistance. Callirhoe, for example, prayed to Aphrodite to give her Chaereas as a husband (*Chaer.* 1.1). Later, when circumstances separated her from Chaereas, she prayed that she would attract no other man (*Chaer.* 2.2). In *An Ephesian Tale*, Anthia petitioned Isis to deliver her or help her remain faithful to her husband (*Eph.* 4.3). Later, after robbers attacked the party, she prayed again: "I pray that I may remain the wife of Habrocomes, even if I have to die or suffer still more than I have already" (*Eph.* 4.5). Anthia prayed multiple times in this story: to Isis, Apis, and Helios. She uttered her petitions openly in temples and shrines.

Women also left records of their prayers in inscriptions devoted to the gods. At the end of her story, Anthia cut her hair and dedicated it to Helios, with this inscription: "On behalf of her husband Habrocomes Anthia dedicated her hair to the god" (*Eph.* 5.11). Her former slaves recognized the names in the inscription and helped to reunite Anthia and Habrocomes. Similar inscriptions have been found in the archaeological record. For example, this Greek inscription was found in Egypt: "To the greatest and highest God, on behalf of Epitychia also called Dionysia and on behalf of her husband Harpochras and their children, in fulfillment of a vow" (*CIJ* 2.1532).[21] This woman, Epitychia, left a marker of her gratitude after an earlier prayer was answered. Both men and women prayed such prayers and left markers of their petitions in temples.[22]

Women also spoke as the recipients of oracles and heavenly messages.[23] Aseneth received a visit from an angel, with whom she conversed at length (*JosAs* 15–16). At the end of the visit, he said to her "the ineffable mysteries of the Most High have been revealed to you" (16.7).[24] In the retelling of Rebekah's story in the Jewish work *Jubilees*, Rebekah had a prophetic dream. She spoke about it to Jacob and predicted her own death (*Jub* 35:6). Greek novels contained similar divine communications. Callhiroe saw in a dream that Chaereas was trying to find her (*Chaer.* 3.7). In *An Ephesian Tale*, Anthia visited the shrine of Apis in Memphis. "This is the most illustrious shrine in Egypt, and the god gives oracles to those who wish them. . . . So Anthia too came and prostrated herself before Apis. 'Kindest of gods,' she prayed, 'who have pity on all strangers, have pity on me too in my misery and make me a true prophecy about Habrocomes.'" In response to her prayer, she received an oracle: "Anthia will soon recover her own husband, Habrocomes" (*Eph.* 5.4).[25] These women made requests for oracles or spoke to others about messages they received from the gods.

Some women served in official religious capacities as prophets. The shrine at Delphi was a famous location known for oracles that were delivered by women on behalf of the gods (see, e.g., Plutarch *Pyth. orac.* 405–406; Valerius Maximus 1.8.10; Pausanias *Descr.* 10.5.5–10). The *Sibylline Oracles* were a written collection of sayings that were identified with female prophets. There were a number of different Sibyls from various places and probably numerous collections of their works. Their prophetic work was well known during this period (e.g., Pausanias *Descr.* 10.12.1–9; Plutarch *Pyth. orac.* 398C–D; Suetonius *Aug.* 31; Tacitus *Ann.* 1.76.1).

SUMMARY

The evidence above suggests that social norms accommodated women's speech in a wide range of locations and on many topics.

Women spoke in communal spaces: temples, markets, harbors, and the assembly. They addressed matters of civic and familial concern, as well as their own well-being. None of these sources apologized for the speech of women. They assumed that the women were doing nothing unusual and often characterized them as virtuous.

This is not to say that women were considered the equals of men in terms of speech. If the subject was political office or legislative and judicial matters, it became much less common to find a woman speaking. The sources presumed that men were rightly in charge of these arenas.

However, women were present in the assembly or courtroom, and occasionally they spoke. Hortensia's speech in the forum was the most formal of these speech events and represented an event that could only have been possible in unusual circumstances for very elite women. Other examples suggested the everyday influence of women. Their speech was part of the communal opinion voiced in the assembly—as, for example, when the city cried out for Callhiroe's presence and lauded her story. Women did not vote or pronounce sentences in these scenes, but they did influence events—as when Callhiroe recognized Chaereas, or when Theocleia advocated Thecla's execution. Women exercised political influence according to cultural norms that made room for their speech.

Two factors seem especially important in the assessment of women's abilities to speak. First, speakers considered the audience they addressed. It was a virtue for people (male and female) to be silent before their social superiors (see chapter 3). But silence was not always a virtue—frankness of speech could also be praised. The key was to know when to speak and when not to. Part of that calculation was an assessment of the social rank of the others involved.

Like everyone, women were expected to calculate their relative social status with regard to those around them. This was a moving target, because social standing, though always hierarchical, had many variables. Society always viewed women as inferior to men in terms of gender, but their social status was also dependent on factors like wealth, citizenship, slave, freed, or free-born status, and their family of origin (see chapter 5). A woman like Junia Rustica might be lower in rank than other men of equal wealth and family origin, but she outranked most of the men of her city. Her speech would likely be expected in some of the civic contexts mentioned in her inscription—as well as in her business dealings, or in relationships with family members, clients, and slaves.

The calculation of social status was more important than the space in which speech took place. Consider a small room off the central atrium in the house of a wealthy but not elite family. In that same space, a woman might have been silent as she listened to her husband negotiate with an important business partner. She might also have consulted with a relative to work together for the political advancement of someone in the family. She would certainly also have ordered slaves, whether male or female, to complete a variety of tasks. The same woman might have done all three of these things outside of her house as well. In such examples, the people involved were more important than the space in the calculation of whether a woman should speak. And the content of the speech, rather than the location, made it political or personal.

The second factor to consider is that women were praised for speeches that embodied traditional virtues—especially the virtue of loyalty to one's family and city.[26] It was certainly possible to criticize women's speech and to evoke ideals of silence as particularly relevant to women. But writers also praised women for speech, and even for bold speech. Plutarch portrayed each of his women as devoted to their families and to the good of their people as a whole. The situations where women negotiated between parties were highly political, but they were often negotiating between their own family members. The remarkable outcome was that the women were able to achieve a solution that furthered the interests of each of the members of the family and those of their city. These concerns were presented as appropriate matters regarding which women could—and even should—speak.

SPEECH AND SILENCE IN
THE NEW TESTAMENT

Many readers of the New Testament today are interested in questions about women's speech. Some New Testament passages sought to restrict women's speech or encourage their silence. Yet other passages displayed women speaking without any apparent disapproval of their actions. As in the other chapters of this book, having a sense of what was expected in the wider culture can help us to imagine how early readers may have received these varied signals.

Two well-known texts of the New Testament seem to discourage or limit women's speech. A portion of 1 Corinthians stated, "Women should be silent in the churches. For they are not permitted to speak, but should be subordinate, as the law also says" (1 Cor 14:34). Similarly, the author of 1 Timothy wrote, "Let a woman learn in silence with full submission. I permit no woman to teach or to have authority over a man; she is to keep silent" (2:11–12). Verses like these conveyed a message that women should not speak.

However, many other passages displayed women speaking with approval. As in other ancient writings, women spoke less frequently than men in the New Testament. However, they were quoted as speaking in a variety of ways. In the Gospels, a number of women characters spoke in ways that were important to the story line. Luke's Gospel presented Mary speaking prophetically before the birth of Jesus. She outlined what God was doing in that moment in light of prior acts of God's faithfulness to Israel (Luke 1:46–55). At the other end of the gospel story, the women at the tomb became the first witnesses to Jesus's resurrection. They shared this experience with the male disciples (Matt 28:1–10; Luke 24:1–11). John's Gospel explicitly quoted Mary Magdalene's message: "I have seen the Lord" (John 20:18).

In some cases, the speech of women was implied rather than directly quoted. Women taught (Acts 18:26), prayed, and prophesied (1 Cor 11:5). They made requests (Mark 7:26) and spoke in the course of their work (Acts 12:13–14). The letters of the New Testament also mentioned women who were deacons (Rom 16:1), apostles (Romans 16:7), and leaders of house churches (e.g., Col 4:15). The titles of these women raise questions about the authority they may have held within the churches, and in particular about their roles as speakers.

Although New Testament texts occasionally enjoined women to silence, there were many more instances in which the speech of women was assumed to be normal or upheld as truthful. This variety makes sense against the background of the complex social conventions of the time. Those norms encouraged self-control, including of speech in the presence of one's social superiors. But they also praised speech that conveyed truth and sought the common good, whether spoken by men or women. The New Testament writings displayed the same variety of social conventions as the culture at large.

Silence as a Virtue

The two New Testament passages that enjoined women to silence reflected the culture's presumption that women were of lower status than men. First Corinthians stated that women "are not permitted to speak but should be subordinate" (14:34). Here, the prohibition against speech was articulated directly in relationship to women's subordinate status. Similarly, 1 Timothy asserted that women should not "teach or have authority over a man; she is to keep silent" (2:12). In that case, silence represented recognition of the differential in cultural authority accorded to men and women.

In 1 Timothy, however, silence was also framed as an exhibition of self-control. The Greek word *sōphrosunē* (self-control or modesty) occurred at the beginning and end of the passage regarding women's behavior (2:9, 15). As I argued in chapter 3, the virtue of modesty often included both dress and speech, as is the case in 1 Tim 2:8–15. The exhortation to silence reflected the gendered social norms of the time. But it was not only a demand for subordination; it was an assertion of the virtue of self-control.

Control of the tongue was a virtue that did not always demand complete silence, even of women. The same virtue was seen in other New Testament texts, including those that assumed the leadership of women. In another part of 1 Timothy, the qualifications for church leaders included self-control with regard to speech. A bishop was to be "an apt teacher" and "not quarrelsome (3:2, 3). Male deacons likewise were to be "not double-tongued" (1 Tim 3:8), and female deacons, "not slanderers" (3:11). False or duplicitous speaking was inappropriate to the life of faith and should disqualify men and women from leadership. The implication was that men and women both spoke, and that good leaders would include those who spoke truthfully.

The qualities of leaders in 1 Tim 3 conveyed the culture's sense that truthful speech was both difficult and virtuous, and it was something to be prized. A person's speech was an expression of his or her nature. The epistle of James conveyed a similar set of expectations about the relationship between speech and a person's character. The same mouth should not bless God and curse those made in God's likeness, for this was duplicitous speech: "Can a fig tree, my brothers and sisters, yield olives, or a grapevine figs?" (Jas 3:12). The underlying idea was that speech exhibited a person's character. The ability to control one's speech thus made sense as a qualification for leadership. The ability to control the tongue suggested the capacity to consider the good of others rather than one's own desires and to weigh relevant factors rather than jumping to conclusions. The examples of women's speech below suggest that women could be recognized as speaking well according to these standards.

Speech on Political Subjects

Some women engaged in speech with political overtones. Their words were recorded without any apparent suggestion of impropriety. For example, Peter's denials of Jesus were prompted by the accusations of a woman. All four Gospels identified as female at least one of the people who questioned Peter about his relationship to Jesus. According to Mark, Peter denied Jesus twice after he was accused by "one of the servant-girls of the high priest" (Mark 14:66, 69). In John, it was the "woman who guarded the gate" (John 18:16) who said to Peter, "'You are not also one of this man's disciples, are you?' He said, 'I am not'" (John 18:17). Each story presented a slave woman of the high priest's household initiating conversation with Peter about his relationship to the accused man, Jesus.

Women occasionally came into view as people who pursued the political and social status of their families. John the Baptist's death resulted when Herod's wife seized an opportunity to have him killed. When Herod promised her daughter "whatever she might ask," she instructed the girl to say "Give me the head of John the Baptist here on a platter" (Matt 14:7–8; cf. Mark 6:25). Having made the promise in front of witnesses at a dinner party, Herod had to follow through or he would have appeared weak. The girl's words were highly political and the fact that she spoke them before others was part of what made them effective.

Persuasion and Advocacy

One other character who sought benefits for family members was the mother of the sons of Zebedee. Matthew's version of the story has the mother of these two disciples making a request: "Declare that these two sons of mine will sit, one at your right hand and one at your left, in your kingdom" (Matt 20:21). She petitioned for the status of her children. Although Jesus rejected the request as "not mine to grant" (20:23), there was nothing unusual about a woman making such a request.

Other women also spoke about or regarding relatives. Elizabeth identified her son's name as John, though it was not a family name (Luke 1:60). Mary scolded the young Jesus for his absence in the temple (Luke 2:48). In a different Gospel, Mary's words initiated Jesus's miracle of making water into wine. She said to Jesus, "They have no wine" (John 2:3). Although he was reluctant and said, "My hour has not yet come" (John 2:4), her next words, "Do whatever he tells you" (John 2:5), expected his response. And indeed, Jesus went on to provide wine (John 2:5–9).

Prayer and Prophecy

Women's prophetic speech was fairly common in New Testament writings. In the Gospel of Luke, both Elizabeth and Mary spoke in ways that identified the presence of God in events around them. Elizabeth was "filled with the Holy Spirit" (Luke 1:41) and said to Mary, "Blessed are you among women, and blessed is the fruit of your womb. And why has this happened to me, that the mother of my Lord comes to me? For as soon as I heard the sound of your greeting, the child in my womb leaped for joy. And blessed is she who believed that there would be a fulfillment of what was spoken to her by the Lord" (Luke 1:42–45). Elizabeth's words conveyed knowledge of God's message to Mary, Mary's pregnancy, and its significance.

Mary's song, the Magnificat, was a response to Elizabeth's greeting. It is another example of prophetic speech in Luke. Mary pointed to God's saving work in history—for example, "He has brought down the powerful from their thrones, and lifted up the lowly" (1:52), and in doing so she positioned Jesus as someone who continued this trajectory of God's action. She also spoke of the future: "From now on all generations will call me blessed" (Luke 1:48).

Another prophet in the early chapters of Luke was Anna, whom Luke identified explicitly as a prophet (Luke 2:36). She lived in the temple and spoke "about the child [Jesus] to all who were looking for the redemption of Jerusalem" (Luke 2:38). Anna's understanding of Jesus's identity even as an infant pointed toward the purpose of his life and ministry.

One interesting case related to prophecy is the dream of Pilate's wife in Matt 27. She sent word to her husband while he was adjudicating Jesus's case: "Have nothing to do with that innocent man, for today I have suffered a great deal because of a dream about him" (27:19). Dreams were often viewed as a form of divine communication, and the interpretation of dreams was similar to prophecy. Pilate's wife interrupted court proceedings to instruct her husband on the basis of a dream she had. Following her intervention, Matthew portrayed Pilate as affirming Jesus's innocence (Matt 27: 23–24).

Prophecy could also be characterized negatively. The imprisonment of Paul and Silas in Philippi resulted when they cast a spirit from a slave girl. She followed them around, saying, "These men are slaves of the Most High God, who proclaim to you a way of salvation" (Acts 16:17). Although her words showed insight into the disciples' identity and mission, Paul and Silas found her annoying. They cast out the spirit, causing her owners to drag them before the local authorities.

Prayers by women were mentioned in passing in the New Testament. Paul referred to both men and women who prayed and prophesied as if these were common occurrences (1 Cor 11:4–5). He argued that women should cover their heads during these types of speech. Acts also included male and female disciples who were constantly devoted to prayer (Acts 1:14). Luke mentioned the prophet Anna's habits of fasting and prayer as part of his description of her as a prophet (Luke 2:37).

CONCLUSION

Modern readers also encounter and interpret language that conveys the value of silence for women alongside evidence that women spoke on a variety of topics and sometimes with authority. Assuming that women never spoke in church as a result of passages like 1 Cor 14:34 or 1 Tim 2:11–12 requires us to ignore a good deal of evidence suggesting that women's speech was common in the culture and even desirable in many circumstances. Instead, a more nuanced approach seems desirable. Some forms of speech by women were likely seen as conventional. Prayer and prophecy by women were so common in both Greek and Jewish sources that no apology or explanation would have been required for these acts. Paul's indication that women should cover their heads when they prayed and prophesied reinforced the idea that these forms of speech were conventional. Participation in parallel forms of speech did not make women equal to men. The social hierarchy between them was preserved in Paul's instructions regarding the head covering (1 Cor 11:3, 7). But women's participation in worship through prayer and prophecy was not something Paul opposed.

Like the culture at large, the New Testament exhibited both evidence of women's speech and social norms of women's subordination and silence. Because of this similarity, my conclusion is that first-century readers would have understood statements about women's silence as rules that they applied according to the conventions of their day. First-century readers were familiar with statements of women's subordination to men and assumptions that they should not speak. It seems quite likely that these readers would have understood New Testament language about women's silence in this way. "They are not permitted to speak" (1 Cor 14:34) may have been read as an affirmation of these social norms. The cultural assumption was that a well-ordered community would prefer the speech of men over that of women. However, given the many situations in which the speech of women was also conventional, prohibition of all speech by women would likely have needed greater explanation—especially because the letter to the Corinthians had already assumed that women's prayer and prophecy was conventional (1 Cor 11). The "rule" of women's silence, as applied by the culture, did not prohibit these forms of speech. Indeed, such speech was encouraged without being perceived as breaking the social norms.

Operating according to these cultural norms, women were likely to assert their social influence by speaking in their own interests and pursuing the needs of their families. Women in the New Testament writings made requests and gave orders. Women of higher status would have expected others—even male church leaders—to respond. Cultural norms gave women and men a variety of venues in which to exercise social, religious, and political influence.

Some women of high status probably also addressed the church in more formal ways. The social conventions suggest that such speech would have been viewed as advantageous as part of the woman's use of her social standing on behalf of others. Her speech would not have been perceived as unacceptable. Someone like Phoebe, whom Paul identified as a "deacon of the church (*ekklesia*) in Cenchreae" (Rom 16:1), was an official representative of her congregation (see chapter 5). As such, her speech would likely have been viewed as consistent with the rules of culture.

The New Testament reflected social norms that viewed women as inferior and insisted upon their silence. However, it also displayed conventions from the same culture suggesting that control of the tongue was an attribute of good leaders. Furthermore, New Testament writings mirrored the social practices that made room for and even encouraged women's speech. Readers of the New Testament today should not assume that the rules of silence applied in every situation where women might speak. A woman whose community accorded her a place of honor could draw on that status to address others. Her speech was likely to have been received with approval.

Chapter 8

Conclusion

IN THIS BOOK, I HAVE PRESENTED and interpreted evidence for the cultural conventions regarding women's roles in the New Testament period. The evidence has affirmed many assumptions modern readers have about ancient women. However, it also highlighted a variety of social practices that allowed and encouraged women's participation.

Some societal norms placed constraints on women. Many sources praised women for subordinating their interests to those of their husbands and families. They suggested that women should be modest, sexually loyal to husbands, and ideally silent. In their application, however, the virtues allowed greater action by women than this description would seem to allow. Women were ideally assigned to the realm of the home, but in practice their industry took them into the streets and markets as they sought the social and economic well-being of their families. Modesty or self-control was not only a domestic virtue but was an important civic virtue in this period. It was a key characteristic of the wise leader, and thus served as a qualification for civic office. Each of the virtues could be enacted in various ways, and each had manifestations that included active involvement in the community.

Some of the legal constraints modern interpreters have imagined were not practiced in this period. Like men, Roman women became legally independent on the death of their fathers, and they stood to inherit some of his property. These women were not under the legal authority of their husbands, and they retained control over some of their property. Although the legal status of non-Roman women is less clear, evidence of women's property ownership in Asia Minor and Egypt suggests some similarities in legal status. Whatever their citizenship, wealthy women often had a great deal of property at their disposal, while lower-class women owned less but wielded similar power over it.

Nevertheless, women's legal status was also a mix of practices. The law required most women to have a guardian for some legal transactions. Men had formal legal status that was not officially granted to women. Yet in many cases women had more freedom to act on their own behalf than the law suggested. Women acted with respect to their property with the same legal powers of male owners. In practice, their guardians had little or no control over their property. Although they did not have the same legal power their husbands did, neither were married women subject to their husband's legal authority.

Women employed their wealth and status in many of the same ways men did. Women did not own as much property as men in this period. But they owned land and buildings, slaves, businesses, and animals in varying amounts. Through their wealth, women gained honor as donors of building projects, or by sponsoring civic organizations, games, and festivals. Women of various class levels participated as patrons. Though less frequent than that of men, their civic leadership as patrons was an expected part of the social landscape. Women's patronage also included making loans, manumitting slaves, and acting as advocates for their clients. These roles were not viewed as extraordinary but were an expected part of everyday life.

Women undertook a variety of occupations. They worked to further the economic standing of their families. Some women owned slaves and directed their labor; other women were slaves themselves. Some women earned wages as laborers. A variety of occupations were traditionally associated with women's household work: women cared for children, worked as midwives and nurses, and managed household property and businesses. They produced excess cloth and food and sold such goods to others in large or small amounts. Women also held jobs that would surprise modern readers. They were gladiators, for example, and managed brick production. They were artisans, merchants, and teachers.

Women spoke in the course of performing these tasks. Depending on the situation, they commanded others, gave instructions, and asked pointed questions. They advocated on their own behalf and that of others. They offered hospitality and sought to curry favor with those in power. Although women's speech was conventional, they could also be criticized for speaking in ways that seemed to overstep their social status.

To modern interpreters, some of the ancient evidence appears highly contradictory. It suggests a variety of tasks, roles, and activities that were conventional for women of the New Testament period. At the same time, the traditional virtues that were widely upheld stated that women were by nature passive and should remain quietly indoors. What is more, the evidence pointed to women who sometimes took on roles that the law seemed to expressly forbid. As property owners, women had many of the rights of the *pater familias*, even though the term was explicitly male. Women held positions as magistrates that the law suggested they could not attain. Women controlled their property interests even though required to have a guardian by law. Women spoke in a variety of contexts though they were idealized as silent.

One of the aims of this book has been to explain how these apparent contradictions may have made sense to people at the time. The modern presumption has been that demands restricting women's actions directly contradicted evidence of women doing these things. Scholars have interpreted the diversity of norms regarding women as evidence of distinct groups who disagreed about women's roles, or as discrete locations where actions by women were or were not allowed, or as actions allowed only by certain women.

I have argued instead that the social norms governing women's behavior were multiple and complex. Cultural norms were often in tension. For example, social standing was extremely important in this period and one way to display status was through the fine dress and jewelry women wore. At the same time, the virtue of modesty or self-control asserted that restraint in the display of such finery was a virtue. Balancing these cultural values was not an all-or-nothing proposition, where individual actors were forced to pick either modesty or social influence. They were values actors drew on as they made decisions and sought to influence events around them.

Widely held conventions like the virtue of modesty were enacted in a variety of ways, depending on factors like the actor's social status, cultural location, and circumstances. A woman might be less inclined to speak forcefully in a group of male peers—unless circumstances warranted her intervention. But women also found themselves in groups where they were among those with the highest status, and in such instances their speech could be expected. A woman might defer to a male patron but also pursue social status through her own patronage of a civic organization.

As a result, we see evidence of women who played different roles and still fulfilled social ideals of feminine behavior. Like Junia Theodora of Corinth, they were advocates for the political and social well-being of their communities even as they were characterized as "living modestly." Like Amymone, they might be idealized as "a stayer at home," though their everyday life—including the pursuit of other virtues—required them to leave the home on a regular basis. The evidence suggested society did not view such active women as abandoning traditional virtues.

Thus, although modern readers think of social norms as restricting women's participation, many conventions of the New Testament period supported and even encouraged the social influence and economic participation of women. Cities and associations sought women as patrons and leaders. Women had considerable authority within their households, and their economic contributions were important. Families also praised women for their wise use of social and political influence.

INTERPRETING THE NEW TESTAMENT

Making historical judgments about the lives of ancient women remains a difficult task that is complicated by a lack of direct evidence. The approach of this book does not overcome all of the problems that are inherent to the task. There are still gaps in the historical record. Much of the evidence consists of texts written by men with their own rhetorical agendas.

Modern interpreters are left with many questions we cannot answer. It is difficult to discern, for example, the precise responsibilities of male or female officeholders in this period. We see only glimpses into familial relationships and are left with questions about how the people in question interacted with one another. We often see only the representation of virtue and wonder about the lived reality.

However, the inquiry of this book may be useful in making modern readers aware of our assumptions. Many interpreters have assumed that women did not play active roles in their communities, that they did not own or manage property, and that they were restricted to the household. Becoming aware that we have made some mistaken assumptions about ancient women may help to renew our attention to this subject and give us cause to look again at the stories and artifacts that pertain to women.

Without these notions, we may discover women in the New Testament acting in ways we did not consider possible. Women spoke in a variety of contexts. They owned property and used it to support the Jesus movement. Their actions would have been taken for granted by ancient readers as a normal part of everyday life, but they have subsequently been made invisible to us by the assumptions that women did not do such things.

Even with a clearer sense of what was possible, however, readers may be left with many questions about the interpretation of New Testament texts. The aim of this book is not to identify a single way to interpret a New Testament text. Multiple good interpretations are possible for any of the passages concerning women. Historical inquiry does not yield a single original meaning to the New Testament but helps to expand our knowledge of possible ways early readers may have encountered these writings.

Nor is a goal of this book to specify what modern Christian readers should conclude about the roles of women in churches today. This book's argument may alter some of the terms of contemporary debates about women's roles. It may evoke new questions about former conclusions that were drawn on the basis of faulty information. However, historical study will not yield a single answer to modern questions about women's leadership because these decisions are not based solely on historical information. They also draw on theological views, ecclesial traditions, and contemporary social concerns. While these questions are worth exploring, they lie outside the scope of this book.

Instead, the book seeks to clarify what would have seemed possible from an ancient perspective and in doing so to activate a new set of questions regarding the activities of women. My hope is that readers will return to the New Testament with the ability to see things that were hidden from view. They may look for evidence of women's property ownership and patronage alongside traditional statements of women's virtue. They may be equipped to ask how women's active participation may have fulfilled the expectations of their culture.

To facilitate the rereading of New Testament texts, I summarize the conclusions of this study that interpreters may want to keep in mind:

1. Ancient readers were familiar with a variety of forms of leadership by women. Ancient readers used cultural knowledge to fill in the gaps left by the author. When the New Testament identified a woman with property or status, readers had cultural knowledge of such patterns that they brought to bear on the story. Modern readers can use insights into what the ancient culture was like to consider the text as a first-century reader might have experienced it.

2. Women's leadership and feminine virtues went hand in hand. Evidence of women's devotion to their families did not preclude them from leading civic and religious

organizations. Indeed, such virtue may have served as a qualification for office. Women could be praised for bold leadership as well as domestic virtue. The presence of one did not cancel out the other. Interpreters may want to consider how these elements of culture fit together for ancient people.

3. Jewish women were similar to other women of the period. Jewish practices were not uniform but varied considerably. Some evidence suggests that Jews had social patterns similar to those of the wider culture—as in the case of Jewish people with Greek dowry arrangements. Some practices were distinctive, like Babatha's polygamous marriage. But Babatha's documents also shared a good deal in common with Greek and Roman practices of the time. She owned property and petitioned the court to secure a guardian for her son.

Christian interpreters have often contrasted ancient Jewish culture with Christian innovations, arguing that Christianity improved upon the dire circumstances of women. This study has found little to no evidence to support this argument. Jewish and Christian women shared both the benefits and restrictions of gender that were found in the wider culture.

4. The restrictions society placed on women were real. In this book I have sought to correct common mistakes that overstated the limitations placed on women in the New Testament period. In doing so, I hope that modern readers may have a fuller sense of women's legal and social capacities. However, it would also be a mistake to suggest that women were not disadvantaged both in law and social practice. Prejudice against women was widespread, and no record remains of any sustained protest against it. The assumption of women's inferiority was reflected in lower education levels and fewer opportunities for women.

Modern interpreters should consider those biases along-side the evidence of women's substantial activity and con-tribution to their communities.

Historical information will never yield answers to all the questions modern readers have. There will always be a good deal about the ancient world that we cannot know for certain. As I mentioned in the introduction, many details about women in the New Testament remain unknown. Was Lydia (Acts 16:14–15) married or unmarried? What was her social status? How wealthy was Joanna, Chuza's wife, who supported Jesus's ministry (Luke 8:3)? What roles did deacons (whether male or female) perform? First Timothy lists the qualifications for office but not the job description. Although the social patterns discussed in the book give readers a better sense of the options that were available to women, they do not lead to a single, definitive answer to questions like these.

Although these unanswered questions will leave some readers feeling unsatisfied, a number of positive assertions emerge from this study. Women in the New Testament shared much in common with the culture at large, which exhibited a prefer-ence for men and viewed women as inferior. Women were ide-ally described as modest, industrious, and loyal to their families and cities. Virtuous women were also leaders of their cities, and held municipal and religious offices. They wielded social and po-litical influence. All of these details are useful as we try to flesh out women's actions in New Testament texts and to avoid mistaken assumptions.

The difficulty we have drawing firm historical conclusions can also help us to reassess some of the previous arguments that rejected women's leadership. It no longer seems wise to conclude that strict standards of feminine virtue canceled out women's capacities for leadership. We should not assume that women were never leaders in early churches. We should not assume that they never taught or always stayed at home. These conclusions push back against some previous work suggesting that many early churches eliminated women's active roles. Women's influence and leadership were expected parts of social and religious life, both in and outside of Christian circles.

NOTES

1. Raymond F. Collins, *1 & 2 Timothy and Titus: A Commentary* (Louisville: Westminster John Knox Press, 2002), 69.
2. Risto Saarinen, *The Pastoral Epistles with Philemon & Jude* (Grand Rapids, Mich.: Brazos Press, 2008), 67.
3. See, e.g., Rosalinde A. Kearsley, "Asiarchs, *Archiereis*, and the *Archiereiai* of Asia," *Greek, Roman and Byzantine Studies* 27 (1986): 183–192.
4. For an introduction to the idea that sex and gender are socially constructed, see, e.g., Caroline Vander Stichele and Todd Penner, *Contextualizing Gender in Early Christian Discourse: Thinking Beyond Thecla* (London: T&T Clark, 2009), 17–27.
5. Thomas Laqueur, *Making Sex: Body and Gender from the Greeks to Freud* (Cambridge, Mass.: Harvard University Press, 1990), 26.
6. Ibid., 62.
7. Ibid., 26.
8. David M. Halperin, *One Hundred Years of Homosexuality and Other Essays on Greek Love* (New York: Routledge, 1990), 26.
9. For a discussion, see Halperin, *One Hundred Years of Homosexuality*, 31–32. See also Craig A. Williams, *Roman Homosexuality: Ideologies of Masculinity in Classical Antiquity* (New York: Oxford University Press, 1999), 15–28.

10. Aristotle claimed that women are colder than men (*Gen. an.* 1.20 [728a]). Elsewhere, however, he noted that the point was disputed (*Part. an.* 2.2 [648a]). Hippocrates also thought females to be colder and wetter than males (*Vict.* 1.27; 1.34). See also the discussion in G. E. R. Lloyd, "The Hot and the Cold, the Dry and the Wet in Greek Philosophy," *Hellenic Studies* 84 (1964): 102–103; Dale B. Martin, *The Corinthian Body* (New Haven: Yale University Press, 1995), 32.

11. Helen King, *Hippocrates' Woman: Reading the Female Body in Ancient Greece* (London: Routledge, 1998), 11. Cf. Brooke Holmes, *Gender: Antiquity and Its Legacy* (New York: Oxford University Press, 2012), 14–75; Helen King, *The One-Sex Body on Trial: The Classical and Early Modern Evidence* (Burlington, Vt: Ashgate, 2013), 1–27.

12. See, e.g., Ovidiu Creanga, ed., *Men and Masculinity in the Hebrew Bible and Beyond* (Sheffield: Sheffield Phoenix Press, 2010); Amy Kalmanofsky, *Gender-Play in the Hebrew Bible: The Ways the Bible Challenges Its Gender Norms* (London: Routledge, 2017); Jessica M. Keady, *Vulnerability and Valour: A Gendered Analysis of Everyday Life in the Dead Sea Scrolls Communities* (London: Bloomsbury T&T Clark, 2017); Stephen D. Moore and Janice Capel Anderson, eds., *New Testament Masculinities* (Atlanta: SBL Press, 2003).

13. In biblical studies, see, e.g., Rhiannon Graybill, *Are We Not Men? Unstable Masculinity in the Hebrew Prophets* (New York: Oxford University Press, 2016), 11–13.

14. See Andrew Wallace-Hadrill, *Rome's Cultural Revolution* (Cambridge: Cambridge University Press, 2008), chap. 1. On the changes in gendered cultural practices, see, e.g., Emily A. Hemelrijk, *Hidden Lives, Public Personae: Women and Civic Life in the Roman West* (New York: Oxford University Press, 2015), 23–24.

15. All translations of Livy are by Evan Sage. Livy, *Histories* (trans. Evan T. Sage, vol. 9; Cambridge, Mass.: Harvard University Press, 1935).

16. Majorie Lightman and William Zeisel, "Univira: An Example of Continuity and Change in Roman Society," *CH* 46 (1977): 19–32 (20).

17. All translations of Suetonius are by Robert Graves. Suetonius, *The Twelve Caesars* (trans. Robert Graves and J. B. Rives; London: Penguin, 2007).
18. An earlier writer, the poet Ovid, also told this story (*Fasti* 4.2911-2328), but he may have shared similar motivations.
19. For discussion, see Ross Kraemer, "Non-Literary Evidence for Jewish Women in Rome and Egypt," in *Rescuing Creusa: New Methodological Approaches to Women in Antiquity* (ed. Marilyn Skinner; Lubbock: Texas Tech University Press, 1987), 85-101. Two important works analyzing inscriptions to women include Riet van Bremen, *The Limits of Participation: Women and Civic Life in the Greek East in the Hellenistic and Roman Periods* (Amsterdam: J. C. Gieben, 1996); Hemelrijk, *Hidden Lives, Public Personae.*
20. See Natalie Boymel Kampen, *Image and Status: Roman Working Women in Ostia* (Berlin: Gebr. Mann, 1981), 131-133.
21. Translated by Jane Rowlandson, ed., *Women and Society in Greek and Roman Egypt: A Sourcebook* (Cambridge: Cambridge University Press, 1998), 178-179.

Chapter 2

1. Philo, *On the Special Laws* (trans. F. H. Colson, LCL; Cambridge, Mass.: Harvard University Press, 1968).
2. Juvenal, *Juvenal and Persius* (trans. Susanna Morton Braund; Cambridge, Mass.: Harvard University Press, 2004), 275-277.
3. Arnold Hugh Martin Jones, *The Greek City from Alexander to Justinian* (Oxford: Clarendon Press, 1940), 175. See also David Magie, *Roman Rule in Asia Minor to the End of the the Third Century after Christ* (2 vols.; Princeton: Princeton University Press, 1950), 1:649. For a discussion, see Riet van Bremen, *The Limits of Participation: Women and Civic Life in the Greek East in the Hellenistic and Roman Periods* (Amsterdam: J. C. Gieben, 1996), 3-4.
4. See Suzanne Dixon, "A Family Business: Women's Role in Patronage and Politics at Rome 80-44 B.C.," *Classica et Mediaevalia* 34 (1983): 91.

5. Ramsay MacMullen, "Woman in Public in the Roman Empire," *Historia* 29, no. 2 (1980): 215.

6. See Zeba Crook, "Honor, Shame, and Social Status Revisited," *JBL* 128 (2009): 591–611.

7. Jouette Bassler, *1 Timothy, 2 Timothy, Titus* (Nashville: Abingdon, 1996), 70.

8. For example, Judith P. Hallett, *Fathers and Daughters in Roman Society: Women and the Elite Family* (Princeton: Princeton University Press, 1984), 28–32.

9. Elisabeth Schüssler Fiorenza, *In Memory of Her: A Feminist Theological Reconstruction of Christian Origins* (New York: Crossroads, 1988), 288–291.

10. Elaine Pagels, *The Gnostic Gospels* (New York: Random House, 1979), chap. 3.

11. Bruce W. Winter, *Roman Wives, Roman Widows: The Appearance of New Women in the Pauline Communities* (Grand Rapids, Mich.: Eerdmans, 2003), 38. Cf. Chapters 2 and 3.

12. See, e.g., Bassler, *1 Timothy*, 94; Schüssler Fiorenza, *In Memory of Her*, 224–225. This argument has also been prominent regarding the later centuries of the early Christian period, when monastic practices took hold and celibacy became possible as an established way of life. See, e.g., Elizabeth A. Clark, *Women in the Early Church* (Collegeville, Minn.: Liturgical Press, 1983).

13. Elizabeth Castelli, "Virginity and Its Meaning for Women's Sexuality in Early Christianity," *JFSR* 2 (1986): 62–88 (84–86).

14. Ross Shepard Kraemer, *Unreliable Witnesses: Religion, Gender, and History in the Greco-Roman Mediterranean* (Oxford: Oxford University Press, 2011), 149.

15. For an excellent discussion of these norms, see Carolyn Osiek and Margaret Y. MacDonald, *A Woman's Place: House Churches in Earliest Christianity* (Minneapolis: Fortress Press, 2006).

16. See Cooper's contrast between Roman notions of "public" and recent discussions such as Jürgen Habermas's influential notion of the "public sphere." Kate Cooper, "Closely Watched Households: Visibility, Exposure and Private Power in the Roman *Domus*," *Past and Present* 197 (2007): 19.

17. Kristina Milnor, *Gender, Domesticity, and the Age of Augustus* (Oxford: Oxford University Press, 2005), 21.

18. Cooper, "Closely Watched Households," 21. Cf. Milnor, *Gender, Domesticity, and the Age of Augustus*, 19–22; Beth Severy, *Augustus and the Family at the Birth of the Roman Empire* (New York: Routledge, 2003), 17–21.

19. Jane F. Gardner, "Women in Business Life: Some Evidence from Puteoli," *Acta Instituti Romani Finlandiae* 22 (1998): 11–27; Susan Treggiari, "Jobs for Women," *American Journal of Ancient History* 1 (1976): 76–104.

20. Harriet Fertik, "Privacy and Power: The *De Clementia* and the Domus Aurea," in *Public and Private in the Roman House and Society* (ed. Kaius Tuori and Laura Nissin; JRA Supplement Series 102; Portsmouth, R.I.: Journal of Roman Archaeology, 2015), 17. Cf. Carolyn Osiek, "The Family in Early Christianity: 'Family Values' Revisited," *CBQ* 58 (1996): 1–25; Milnor, *Gender, Domesticity, and the Age of Augustus*, 103; Osiek and MacDonald, *A Woman's Place*, 3–4.

21. Cooper, "Closely Watched Households," 12; Michele George, "Repopulating the Roman House," in *The Roman Family in Italy: Status, Sentiment, Space* (ed. Beryl Rawson and Paul Weaver; Oxford: Clarendon Press, 1997), 300; Richard P. Saller, "*Familia, Domus*, and the Roman Conception of the Family," *Phoenix* 38 (1984): 352.

22. The arguments about the use of household space are similar on this point across diverse locations. See, e.g., George, "Repopulating the Roman House," 299–319; Eric M. Meyers, "The Problems of Gendered Space in Syro-Palestinian Domestic Architecture: The Case of Roman-Period Galilee," in *Early Christian Families in Context: An Interdisciplinary Dialogue* (ed. David L. Balch and Carolyn Osiek; Grand Rapids, Mich.: William B. Eerdmans, 2003), 59–60; Monika Trümper, "Material and Social Environment of Greco-Roman Households in the East: The Case of Hellenistic Delos," in *Early Christian Families in Context: An Interdisciplinary Dialogue* (ed. David L. Balch and Carolyn Osiek; Grand Rapids, Mich.: William B. Eerdmans, 2003), 28–29; Andrew Wallace-Hadrill, "The Social Structure of the Roman House," *Papers of the British School at Rome* 56 (1988): 50–51, 58–77.

23. Some of this and the following section are revised portions of Susan E. Hylen, *A Modest Apostle: Thecla and the History of*

Women in the Early Church (New York: Oxford University Press, 2015), chap. 1.

24. This discussion draws on Pierre Bourdieu, *Outline of a Theory of Practice* (trans. Richard Nice; Cambridge: Cambridge University Press, 1977). See also Charles Taylor, "To Follow a Rule . . ." in *Bourdieu: Critical Perspectives* (ed. Craig Calhoun, Edward LiPuma, and Moishe Postone; Chicago: University of Chicago Press, 1993), 45-60; Kathryn Tanner, *Theories of Culture: A New Agenda for Theology* (Guides to Theological Inquiry; Minneapolis: Fortress Press, 1997).

25. Michel de Certeau, *The Practice of Everyday Life* (trans. Steven Rendall; Berkeley: University of California Press, 1984), xi.

26. Ann Swidler, *Talk of Love: How Culture Matters* (Chicago: University of Chicago Press, 2001), 24.

27. Bourdieu describes his concept of *habitus* as "durable, transposable dispositions." Bourdieu, *Outline of a Theory of Practice*, 72. Cf. Ted A. Smith, *The New Measures: A Theological History of Democratic Practice* (Cambridge: Cambridge University Press, 2007), 27-28, 75-78; de Certeau, *The Practice of Everyday Life*, 29.

28. For example, see Peter Richardson, "Early Synagogues as Collegia in the Disapora and Palestine," in *Voluntary Associations in the Greco-Roman World* (ed. John S. Kloppenborg and Stephen G. Wilson; London: Routledge, 1996), 90-109; John S. Kloppenborg, "Edwin Hatch, Churches and *Collegia*," in *Origins and Method: Towards a New Understanding of Christianity and Judaism* (ed. Bradley H. McLean; JSNTSupp 86; Sheffield: Sheffield Academic Press, 1993), 212-238; Philip A. Harland, "Familial Dimension of Group Identity (II): 'Mothers' and 'Fathers' in Associations and Synagogues of the Greek World," *Journal for the Study of Judaism* 38 (2007): 57-79.

29. For a discussion of women's leadership in house churches, see Osiek and MacDonald, *A Woman's Place*, 144-219; Carolyn Osiek, "The Patronage of Women in Early Christianity," in *A Feminist Companion to Patristic Literature* (ed. Amy-Jill Levine; New York: T & T Clark, 2008), 173-192.

30. Severy, *Augustus and the Family*; Kristina Milnor, *Gender, Domesticity, and the Age of Augustus: Inventing Private Life* (Oxford: Oxford University Press, 2005).

31. Milnor, *Gender, Domesticity, and the Age of Augustus*, 83.

32. The autobiography is thought to be the foundation of Nicolaus of Damascus's work. See, e.g., *FGrH* F 127.3-8. 128.13-15.
33. Jo Ann McNamara, "Gendering Virtue," in *Plutarch's Advice to the Bride and Groom and a Consolation to His Wife: English Translations, Commentary, Interpretive Essays, and Bibliography* (ed. Sarah B. Pomeroy; New York: Oxford University Press, 1999), 151-161, at 153.
34. Severy, *Augustus and the Family*, 55.
35. Severy, *Augustus and the Family*, 134
36. Livy *Ab Urbe Condita* 2.40.1-12; Dionysius of Halicarnassus, *Ant. rom.* 8.39-54. Cf. Severy, *Augustus and the Family*, 131-138; Susan E. Wood, *Imperial Women: A Study in Public Images, 40 B.C.-A.D. 68* (Leiden: Brill, 1999), 78.
37. Eve D'Ambra wrote that this is "surely a statement in which ideology mastered reality." D'Ambra, 60. Cf. Judith P. Hallett, "Perspectives on Roman Women," in *From Augustus to Nero: The First Dynasty of Imperial Rome* (ed. Ronald Mellor; East Lansing: Michigan State University Press, 1990), 141.
38. Ovid, *Ex Ponto* (trans. Arthur Leslie Wheeler; New York: G. P. Putnam's Sons, 1924). Cf. Ovid *Pont.* 4.13.29; Val Max. 6.1; Horace *Carm.* 3.14.5; Cassius Dio 58.2.4-6.

Chapter 3

1. Translations of *Advice to the Bride and Groom* are by Russell. Plutarch, "Advice to the Bride and Groom," in *Plutarch's Advice to the Bride and Groom and A Consolation to His Wife: English Translations, Commentary, Interpretive Essays, and Bibliography* (ed. Sarah B. Pomeroy; New York: Oxford University Press, 1999), 5-13.
2. Plutarch, *Moralia* (trans. Frank Cole Babbitt, 1; New York: G. P. Putnam's Sons, 1927). Similar ideas are found in Diogenes Laertius 1.70; Philo, *Fug.* 14.126; Plutarch, *Garr.* 1, 4, 17.
3. Translations of *De Garrulitate* are by Hembold. Plutarch, *Moralia* (trans. W. C. Helmbold, 6; Cambridge, Mass.: Harvard University Press, 2005).
4. Rebecca Langlands, *Sexual Morality in Ancient Rome* (Cambridge: Cambridge University Press, 2006), 2.

5. Translations of Valerius Maximus are by Bailey. Valerius Maximus, *Memorable Doings and Sayings* (trans. D. R. Shackelton Bailey, vol. 2; Cambridge, Mass.: Harvard University Press, 2000), 3.

6. Livy, *Histories* (trans. B. O. Foster, vol. 1; Cambridge, Mass.: Harvard University Press, 1919), 199.

7. *RIC* 2.135, 176–178, 343. On the *pudicitia* of men, see also Langlands, *Sexual Morality*, 281–293.

8. Translated by Mary R. Lefkowitz and Maureen B. Fant, *Women's Life in Greece and Rome: A Source Book in Translation* (2nd ed.; Baltimore: Johns Hopkins University Press, 1992), 18.

9. Translated by Jo-Ann Shelton, *As the Romans Did* (2nd ed.; New York: Oxford University Press, 1998), 292.

10. See, e.g., Susan Treggiari, "Jobs for Women," *American Journal of Ancient History* 1 (1976): 76–104.

11. For example, *P.Fay.* 91; *P.Oxy.* 6.932; 31.2593; 33.2680; *Stud. Pal.* 22.40.

12. For example, *BGU* 4.1058; *P.Oxy.* 1.91

13. For example, *CIL* 5.7763; 6.3604; 6.13299; 6.13303; 6.25392; 6.31711; Propertius 4.11.36; Plutarch, *Ti. C. Gracch.* 1.7.

14. Translated by Shelton, *As the Romans Did*, 293.

15. For discussion of *pietas*, see also Richard P. Saller, *Patriarchy, Property, and Death in the Roman Family* (Cambridge: Cambridge University Press, 1994), 105–114.

16. For the Greek texts and translation, see Rosalinde A. Kearsley, "Women and Public Life in Imperial Asia Minor: Hellenistic Tradition and Augustan Ideology," *Ancient West and East* 4 (2005): 189–211 (203–208). For additional examples of women praised for civic and domestic virtues, see Pleket 13; *CIL* 9.4894; 10.5069; 11.405; 11.5270. In Latin honorary inscriptions, women were most often praised using the same vocabulary as male honorees. See Elizabeth P. Forbis, *Municipal Virtues in the Roman Empire: The Evidence of Italian Honorary Inscriptions* (Stuttgart: B. G. Teubner, 1996), 85.

17. Contra, e.g., Jouette Bassler, *1 Timothy, 2 Timothy, Titus* (Nashville: Abingdon, 1996), 97–98; Deborah Krause, *1 Timothy* (London: T&T Clark, 2004), 104–106. See also my argument in Susan E. Hylen, *A Modest Apostle: Thecla and the History of*

Women in the Early Church (New York: Oxford University Press, 2015) 43–45, 56–65.

Chapter 4

1. Jane F. Gardner, "Gender-Role Assumptions in Roman Law," *Echos du Monde Classique* 39 (1995): 377–400 (377).
2. Richard P. Saller, "Pater Familias, Mater Familias, and the Gendered Semantics of the Roman Household," *Classical Philology* 94, no. 2 (1999): 182–197 (182–185).
3. Translated by Judith Evans Grubbs, *Women and the Law in the Roman Empire: A Sourcebook on Marriage, Divorce, and Widowhood* (London: Routledge, 2002), 25.
4. Ibid., 29.
5. Ibid., 89.
6. See Suzanne Dixon, *The Roman Mother* (Norman: University of Oklahoma Press, 1988), 62–63.
7. See Susan Treggiari, "Divorce Roman Style: How Easy and How Frequent Was It?," in *Marriage, Divorce, and Children in Ancient Rome* (ed. Beryl Rawson; Oxford: Clarendon Press, 1991), 32; Richard P. Saller, "Men's Age at Marriage and Its Consequences in the Roman Family," *CP* 82 (1987): 33.
8. See the discussion by Susan Treggiari, *Roman Marriage: Iusti Coniuges from the Time of Cicero to the Time of Ulpian* (Oxford: Clarendon Press, 1991), 233–258.
9. Martial, *Epigrams* (trans. D. R. Shackelton Bailey, Loeb Classical Library 95; Cambridge, Mass.: Harvard University Press, 1993). Cf. Plutarch, *Conj. praec.* 14.
10. Dixon, *Roman Mother*, 44.
11. *Rules of Ulpian* 15.1–3. See Evans Grubbs, *Women and the Law*, 84; Thomas A. J. McGinn, *Prostitution, Sexuality, and the Law in Ancient Rome* (New York: Oxford University Press, 1998), 70–84.
12. Kristina Milnor, *Gender, Domesticity, and the Age of Augustus* (Oxford: Oxford University Press, 2005), 153.
13. See the discussion by Evans Grubbs, *Women and the Law*, 38–42.
14. Tacitus, *Agricola* (trans. M. Hutton and R. M. Oglivie; Cambridge, Mass.: Harvard University Press, 1970).

15. See the discussion of marital virtues in Treggiari, *Roman Marriage*, 229–261.
16. Cf. Cicero *Off.* 1.54–55.
17. *P.Yadin* 10, 14–19, 26. For texts and translation, see Ross Shepard Kraemer, *Women's Religions in the Greco-Roman World: A Sourcebook* (Oxford: Oxford University Press, 2004), 143–152.
18. Oudshoorn disagrees that Babatha's marriage was necessarily polygamous, arguing that Miriam may have previously divorced Judah. See Jacobine G. Oudshoorn, *The Relationship between Roman and Local Law in the Babatha and Salome Komaise Archives: General Analysis and Three Case Studies on Law of Succession, Guardianship and Marriage* (Leiden: Brill, 2007), 11, 393.
19. For discussion, see Adiel Schremer, "How Much Jewish Polygyny in Roman Palestine?," *PAAJR* 63 (1997–2001): 181–223.
20. See the discussion of *DJD* 2.115, *P.Yadin* 18 and 37 by Hannah Cotton, "A Cancelled Marriage Contract from the Judean Desert," *JRS* 84 (1994): 64–86; Oudshoorn, *Relationship between Roman and Local Law*. See also Tal Ilan, "Women's Archives in the Judean Desert," *The Dead Sea Scrolls Fifty Years after Their Discovery* (Lawrence Schiffman, Emanuel Tob, and James C. VanderKam eds.; Jerusalem: Israel Exploration Society, 2000), 758.
21. See, e.g., *P.Mich.* 2.121 recto 4.1 (*BL* 6.80). For the return of the dowry, see *BGU* 4.1105; 8. 1848.
22. See, e.g., *P.Kron.* 52.
23. For a discussion of the familial expectations and many examples, see Riet van Bremen, *The Limits of Participation: Women and Civic Life in the Greek East in the Hellenistic and Roman Periods* (Amsterdam: J. C. Gieben, 1996).
24. The Latin term for slave marriage was *contubernium*. See Evans Grubbs, *Women and the Law*, 138–139, 143–145; Treggiari, *Roman Marriage*, 52–54.
25. See the discussion by Charles L. Babcock, "The Inscriptions," in *The Collection of Antiquities of the American Academy in Rome* (ed. Larissa Bonfante and Helen Nagy; Ann Arbor: University of Michigan Press, 2015), 96–98.
26. Translated by Dale B. Martin, "Slave Families and Slaves in Families," in *Early Christian Families in Context: An*

Interdisciplinary Dialogue (ed. David L. Balch and Carolyn Osiek; Grand Rapids, Mich.: William B. Eerdmans, 2003), 211.

27. With the exception that those in the senatorial class could not marry freedpeople.

28. Treggiari, "Divorce Roman Style," 31–46 (45).

29. Fathers initially had the authority to dissolve their daughter's marriages and marry them to another man. Over time the law clarified that a father could not dissolve his daughter's marriage without her consent. Ulpian, *Dig.* 43.30.1.5.

30. McGinn, *Prostitution, Sexuality, and the Law*, 171–172.

31. David Instone Brewer, "Jewish Women Divorcing Their Husbands in Early Judaism: The Background to Papyrus Se'elim 13," *HTR* 92 (1999): 349–357.

32. Richard P. Saller, *Patriarchy, Property, and Death in the Roman Family* (Cambridge: Cambridge University Press, 1994), 68.

33. In addition to the discussion by Saller (*Patriarchy, Property, and Death in the Roman Family*), see Jens-Uwe Krause, *Witwen und Waisen im Römischen Reich, 1: Verwitwung und Wiederverheiratung* (vol. 1; Stuttgart: Franz Steiner Verlag, 1994), 7–107.

34. Cicero, *Pro Caelio* (trans. R. Gardner; Cambridge, Mass.: Harvard University Press, 1958).

35. For example, Musonius Rufus, *Frag.* 15–16; Plutarch, *Frat. amor.* 4 (479E–480A). On the reciprocal nature of piety, see Richard P. Saller, "*Pietas*, Obligation and Authority in the Roman Family," in *Alte Geschichte und Wissenschaftsgeschichte: Festschrift für Karl Christ zum 65. Geburtstag* (ed. Peter Kneissl and Volker Losemann; Darmstade: Wissenschaftliche Buchgesellschaft, 1988), 393–410.

36. Sammelbuch 6263. For a translation, see Jo-Ann Shelton, *As the Romans Did* (2nd ed.; New York: Oxford University Press, 1998), 23.

37. See, e.g., Dixon, *Roman Mother*, chap. 7.

38. April Pudsey, "Death and the Family: Widows and Divorcées in Roman Egypt," in *Families in the Roman and Late Antique Roman World* (ed. Mary Harlow and Lena Larsson Lonén; New York: Continuum, 2012), 157–180 (165).

39. Elsewhere I argue against the common scholarly assumption that Christian women sought autonomy by remaining unmarried.

Susan E. Hylen, *A Modest Apostle: Thecla and the History of Women in the Early Church* (New York: Oxford University Press, 2015), 31–42.

40. In using the language "it is not lawful for you to have your brother's wife" (Mark 6:18), Mark's wording seems to lean in this direction.

41. For a discussion, see, e.g., Abraham J. Malherbe, "How to Treat Old Women and Old Men: The Use of Philosophical Traditions and Scripture in 1 Timothy 5," in *Scripture and Traditions* (ed. Patrick Gray and Gail R. O'Day; Leiden: Brill, 2008), 281, 285; Benjamin Fiore, *The Pastoral Epistles: First Timothy, Second Timothy, Titus* (SP 12; Collegeville, Minn.: Liturgical Press, 2007), 102; Luke Timothy Johnson, *The First and Second Letters to Timothy: A New Translation with Introduction and Commentary* (New York: Doubleday, 2001), 260–261, 277–278.

42. For example, Jouette Bassler, *1 Timothy, 2 Timothy, Titus* (Nashville: Abingdon, 1996), 98; Deborah Krause, *1 Timothy* (London: T&T Clark, 2004), 104; David A. Ackerman, *1&2 Timothy, Titus* (Kansas City, Mo.: Beacon Hill Press, 2016), 211–212.

43. For this view, see, e.g., Krause, *1 Timothy*, 103; Margaret Davies, *The Pastoral Epistles* (Sheffield: Sheffield Academic Press, 1996), 86.

Chapter 5

1. Willem M. Jongman, "The Early Roman Empire: Consumption," in *The Cambridge Economic History of the Greco-Roman World* (ed. Walter Scheidel, Ian Morris, and Richard Saller; Cambridge: Cambridge University Press, 2007), 592–618 (597).

2. Translated by Alison E. Cooley, "Women Beyond Rome: Trend Setters or Dedicated Followers of Fashion?," in *Women and the Roman City in the Latin West* (ed. Emily A. Hemelrijk and Greg Woolf; Leiden: Brill, 2013), 33.

3. Emily A. Hemelrijk, *Hidden Lives, Public Personae: Women and Civic Life in the Roman West* (New York: Oxford University Press, 2015); Emily A. Hemelrijk, "Female Munificence in the Cities of the Latin West," in *Women and the Roman City in the Latin*

West (ed. Emily A. Hemelrijk and Greg Woolf; Leiden: Brill, 2013), 65–84.

4. For a discussion and this estimate, see Riet van Bremen, *The Limits of Participation: Women and Civic Life in the Greek East in the Hellenistic and Roman Periods* (Amsterdam: J. C. Gieben, 1996), 108–112. See also Riet van Bremen, "A Family from Sillyon," *ZPE* 104 (1994): 43–56.

5. Translated by Jane Rowlandson, ed., *Women and Society in Greek and Roman Egypt: A Sourcebook* (Cambridge: Cambridge University Press, 1998), 170.

6. *Epigraphica* 1 (1939) 160–162. See the discussion by Suzanne Dixon, "A Woman of Substance: Iunia Libertas of Ostia," *Helios* 19 (1992): 162–174.

7. Ilse Mueller, "Women in the Roman Funerary Inscriptions," *ZPE* 175 (2010): 295–303.

8. Plutarch, *Moralia* (trans. Harold North Fowler, 10; Cambridge, Mass.: Harvard University Press, 2005), 145–147.

9. For discussion, see, e.g., van Bremen, *Limits*, 32.

10. Carolyn Osiek, "Family Matters," in *Christian Origins* (ed. Richard A. Horsley; Minneapolis: Fortress Press, 2005), 212. See also Zeba Crook, "Honor, Shame, and Social Status Revisited," 128 (2009): 591–611.

11. See Cassius Dio *Hist.* 57.12, 16; 58.2.

12. Ovid *Fasti* 6.637–640. See also Beth Severy, *Augustus and the Family at the Birth of the Roman Empire* (New York: Routledge, 2003), 131–134.

13. See, e.g., Rosalinde A. Kearsley, "Women and Public Life in Imperial Asia Minor: Hellenistic Tradition and Augustan Ideology," *Ancient West and East* 4 (2005): 91–121.

14. Translated by Hemelrijk, *Hidden Lives, Public Personae*, 159.

15. *SEG* 18.143, Inscription 1. For the full inscriptions with translations, see Rosalinde A. Kearsley, "Women in Public Life in the Roman East: Iunia Theodora, Claudia Metrodora and Phoebe, Benefactress of Paul," *TynBul* 50 (1999): 189–211 (203–208).

16. *SEG* 18.143, Inscription 5.

17. R. Merkelbach and S. Sahin, "Die publizierten Inschriften von Perge," *EA* 11 (1988): 119–120.

18. For example, compare the inscription honoring Claudia Metrodora. Jeanne Robert and Louis Robert, "Bulletin

épigraphique," *Revue des études grecques* 69 (1956) 152–153 (no. 213). For discussion, see van Bremen, *Limits*, 84 n. 3.
19. Translated by Bernadette J. Brooten, *Women Leaders in the Ancient Synagogue: Inscriptional Evidence and Background Issues* (Chico, Calif.: Scholars Press, 1982), 5. See also the inscription to Sara Ura the elder (*CIJ* 1.400); Brooten, *Women Leaders in the Ancient Synagogue*, 45.
20. Translated by Brooten, *Women Leaders in the Ancient Synagogue*, 159. For a range of donations, see pp. 157–165.
21. Jane F. Gardner, "Women in Business Life: Some Evidence from Puteoli," *Acta Instituti Romani Finlandiae* 22 (1998): 21.
22. For example, *TPSulp.* 82, 62. For a discussion of lending practices in Puteoli, see Gardner, "Women in Business Life," 11–27.
23. Evidence of women owning slaves is seen in *P.Oxy.* 34.2713; 50.3555; *P.Oxy. Hels* 26. Women also freed slaves *P.Oxy.* 38.2843.
24. Author's translation.
25. See Kevin Madigan and Carolyn Osiek, *Ordained Women in the Early Church: A Documentary History* (Baltimore: Johns Hopkins University Press, 2005).

Chapter 6

1. Translated by Mary R. Lefkowitz and Maureen B. Fant, *Women's Life in Greece and Rome: A Source Book in Translation* (2nd ed.; Baltimore: Johns Hopkins University Press, 1992), 223.
2. See Richard P. Saller, *Patriarchy, Property, and Death in the Roman Family* (Cambridge: Cambridge University Press, 1994), chap. 2.
3. For example, Valerius Maximus, 7.7.4; Suetonius, *Divus Julius* 52; *P.Mich.* 7.434.
4. For discussion, see Keith Hopkins, "Contraception in the Roman Empire," *Comparative Studies in Society and History* 8 (1965): 124–151. See also Angus McLaren, *A History of Contraception: From Antiquity to the Present Day* (Oxford: Basil Blackwell, 1990), 42–72.
5. For example, Ovid, *Amores* 2.13, 2.14; Seneca, *Helv.* 16. See also Soranus, *Gynecology* 1.19.60.
6. Translated by Roger S. Bagnall and Raffaella Cribiore, *Women's Letters from Ancient Egypt, 300 BC–AD 800* (Ann Arbor: University of Michigan Press, 2006), 169.

7. Cicero, *Tusculan Disputations* (trans. J. E. King, LCL 141; Cambridge, Mass.: Harvard University Press, 1945). A later source, speaking of the second-century emperor Marcus Aurelius, also suggests that it was habitual to bring children up with nurses: "As soon as he passed beyond the age when children are brought up under the care of nurses he was handed over to advanced instructors" (*Historia Augusta,* Marcus 2.1). *Historia Augusta* (trans. David Magie, LCL 139; Cambridge, Mass.: Harvard Univeristy Press, 1921).

8. For example, *CIL* 6.5201, 34383. For discussion, see Keith R. Bradley, "Wet-nursing at Rome: A Study in Social Relations," in *The Family in Ancient Rome* (ed. Beryl Rawson; Ithaca, N.Y.: Cornell University Press, 1986), 202–213.

9. Translated by Lefkowitz and Fant, *Women's Life,* 222.

10. Aulus Gellius, *Attic Nights* (trans. John C. Rolfe; Cambridge, Mass.: Harvard University Press, 1927), 355.

11. For example, Tacitus, *Dialogues* 28.

12. Tacitus, *Dialogues on Oratory* (trans. W. Peterson and M. Winterbottom; Cambridge, Mass.: Harvard University Press, 1970).

13. See Sandra R. Joshel, "Nurturing the Master's Child: Slavery and the Roman Child-Nurse," *Signs* 12, no. 1 (1986): 3–22.

14. Alan K. Bowman, "Literacy in the Roman Empire: Mass and Mode," in *Literacy in the Roman World* (ed. J. H. Humphrey; Journal of Roman Archaeology Supplement Series 3; Ann Arbor: Journal of Roman Archaeology, 1991), 123.

15. Bagnall and Cribiore, *Women's Letters,* 48–49, 60–67; Beryl Rawson, *Children and Childhood in Roman Italy* (Oxford: Oxford University Press, 2003), 197–207; Ann Ellis Hanson, "Ancient Illiteracy," in *Literacy in the Roman World* (ed. J. H. Humphrey; Journal of Roman Archaeology Supplement Series 3; Ann Arbor: Journal of Roman Archaeology, 1991), 159–198; Raffaella Cribiore, *Gymnastics of the Mind: Greek Education in Hellenistic and Roman Egypt* (Princeton: Princeton University Press, 2001), chap. 3.

16. On the misinterpretation of the *vilica* as the wife of the *vilicus,* see Ulrike Roth, "Inscribed Meaning: The Vilica and the Villa Economy," *Papers of the British School at Rome* 72 (2004): 101–124.

17. Translated by Jane Rowlandson, ed., *Women and Society in Greek and Roman Egypt: A Sourcebook* (Cambridge: Cambridge University Press, 1998), 236.
18. Translated by Bagnall and Cribiore, *Women's Letters*, 283.
19. See the discussion by Bagnall and Cribiore, *Women's Letters*, 283.
20. Elaine Fantham et al., *Women in the Classical World: Image and Text* (trans. Natalie Kampen; New York: Oxford University Press, 1994), 334.
21. Translated by Bagnall and Cribiore, *Women's Letters*, 186.
22. See also Tapio Helen, *Organization of Roman Brick Production in the First and Second Centuries A.D.: An Interpretation of Roman Brick Stamps* (Helsinki: Academia Scientiarum Fennica, 1975), 112–113.
23. Päivi Setälä, "Women and Brick Production—Some New Aspects," in *Women, Wealth and Power in the Roman Empire* (ed. Päivi Setälä, et al.; 25; Rome: Acta Instituti Romani Finlandiae, 2002), 187.
24. Ibid., 186, 200.
25. *P.Grenf.* 1.45a (BL 3.75, 9.96), *M.Chr.* 260; *P.Aberd.* 30 (*BL* 3.211). See the discussion by Rowlandson, ed., *Women and Society in Greek and Roman Egypt: A Sourcebook*, 253.
26. Fantham et al., *Women in the Classical World*, 336–337.
27. Roth, "Inscribed Meaning," 101–102.
28. Susan Treggiari, "Jobs for Women," *Americal Journal of Ancient History* 1 (1976): 76–104.
29. Susan Treggiari, "Jobs in the Household of Livia," *PBSR* 43 (1975): 61.
30. See discussion in Rowlandson, ed., *Women and Society in Greek and Roman Egypt: A Sourcebook*, 269; Bagnall and Cribiore, *Women's Letters*, 353–354.
31. See also Claire Holleran, "Women and Retail in Roman Italy," in *Women and the Roman City in the Latin West* (ed. Emily Hemelrijk and Greg Woolf; Leiden: Brill, 2013), 313–330; Treggiari, "Jobs," 76–104.
32. Miriam Beth Peskowitz, *"The Work of Her Hands": Gendering Everyday Life in Roman-Period Judaism in Palestine (70–250 C.E.), Using Textile Production as a Case* (Ann Arbor: UMI Dissertation Services, 1993), 59–60.
33. Translated by Lefkowitz and Fant, *Women's Life*, 216.

34. Cf. Tacitus, *Ann.* 15.32.3; Dio Cassius, *Hist.* 67.8.4, 76.16.1; Suetonius, *Domitian* 4.2.
35. Translated by Lefkowitz and Fant, *Women's Life*, 222.
36. For example, *P.Gen.* 2.103; *Pleket* 12.G; *CIL* 6.9614-9619.

Chapter 7

1. Translations of Livy are by Sage. Livy, Histories (trans. Evan T. Sage, vol. 9; Cambridge: Harvard University Press, 1935), 417.
2. Translation by Braund. Juvenal, *Juvenal and Persius* (trans. Susanna Morton Braund; Cambridge, Mass.: Harvard University Press, 2004), 275-277.
3. Translations of Plutarch's *Advice* are by Donald Russell. Plutarch, "Advice to the Bride and Groom," in *Plutarch's Advice to the Bride and Groom and A Consolation to His Wife: English Translations, Commentary, Interpretive Essays, and Bibliography* (ed. Sarah B. Pomeroy; New York: Oxford University Press, 1999), 10.
4. For example, Plutarch *Garr.* 23; *Conj. praec.* 32; Livy, *Hist.* 34.5.12-13.
5. Translations of the *Lives* are by Perrin. Plutarch, *Lives* (trans. Bernadotte Perrin; Cambridge, Mass.: Harvard University Press, 1921).
6. Apuleius, *Metamorphoses* (trans. J. Arthur Hanson, LCL 44; Cambridge, Mass.: Harvard University Press), 51.
7. Plutarch, *Bravery of Women* (trans. Frank Cole Babbitt; Cambridge, Mass.: Harvard University Press, 1931).
8. Appian, *Roman History* (trans. Horace White; New York: Macmillan, 1913), 199. I am grateful to Bart Bruehler for bringing this example to my attention.
9. See Bradley Buszard, "The Speech of Greek and Roman Women in Plutarch's Lives," *Classical Philology* 105, no. 1 (2010): 83-115 (84-86). The other speeches considered here are Plutarch, *Rom.* 19 (Hersilia); *Cor.* 33-36 (Valeria and Volumnia); *Pomp.* 74. (Cornelia); *Dion* 21 (Theste); *Dion* 51; (Aristomache); *Ant.* 35 (Octavia); *Cleom.* 22 (Cratesicleia); *Ti. C. Gracch.* 15 (Licinnia).
10. Porcia's acts stood alongside other stories of women whose bravery spurred their family on to equal or greater acts of loyalty

to family and state. For example, *Ti. C. Gracch.* 15, Licinia; *Cleom.* 22, Cratiscleia.

11. See also *Leukippe and Kleitophon* 8.13–15; *Daphn.* 2.15–16.

12. See also Emily A. Hemelrijk, "Female Munificence in the Cities of the Latin West," in *Women and the Roman City in the Latin West* (ed. Emily A. Hemelrijk and Greg Woolf; Leiden: Brill, 2013); Riet van Bremen, *The Limits of Participation: Women and Civic Life in the Greek East in the Hellenistic and Roman Periods* (Amsterdam: J. C. Gieben, 1996).

13. Emily A. Hemelrijk, *Hidden Lives, Public Personae: Women and Civic Life in the Roman West* (New York: Oxford University Press, 2015), 159.

14. Ibid. For an additional analysis of this inscription, see John F. Donahue, "Iunia Rustica of Cartima: Female Munificence in the Roman West," *Latomus* 63 (2004): 873–891.

15. Hemelrijk, *Hidden Lives, Public Personae*, 160.

16. Translated by Roger S. Bagnall and Raffaella Cribiore, *Women's Letters from Ancient Egypt: 300 BC–AD 800* (Ann Arbor: University of Michigan Press, 2006), 172.

17. Ibid., 314.

18. Ibid., 283.

19. See, e.g., Markus McDowell, *Prayers of Jewish Women: Studies of Patterns of Prayer in the Second Temple Period* (WUNT 211; Tübingen: Mohr Siebeck, 2006).

20. Pseudo-Philo, "Biblical Antiquities," in *The Old Testament Pseudepigrapha* (ed. James H. Charlesworth; vol. 2; New York: Doubleday, 1985), 364.

21. William Horbury and David Noy, *Jewish Inscriptions of Graeco-Roman Egypt* (Cambridge: Cambridge University Press, 1992), 199–201. The phrase "greatest and highest God" may point to her Jewish identity, though this point is debated.

22. See, e.g., Jill Marshall's discussion of the temple of Artemis in Corinth. Jill Marshall, *Women Praying and Prophesying: Gender and Inspired Speech in First Corinthians* (Atlanta: Emory University, Electronic Theses and Dissertations, 2015), chaps. 2 and 4.

23. See also Randall D. Chesnutt, "Revelatory Experiences Attributed to Biblical Women in Early Jewish Literature," in *"Women Like*

This": *New Perspectives on Jewish Women in the Greco-Roman World* (ed. Amy-Jill Levine; Atlanta: Scholars Press, 1991).

24. Translation by Burchard. "Joseph and Aseneth," in *The Old Testament Pseudepigrapha* (ed. James H. Charlesworth, 2 vols.; New York: Doubleday, 1985), 228–229.

25. Translation by Anderson. Xenophon of Ephesus, "An Ephesian Tale," in *Collected Ancient Greek Novels* (ed. B. P. Reardon; Berkeley: University of California Press, 1989), 161.

26. On gendered virtues, see chapter 3. See also Susan E. Hylen, *A Modest Apostle: Thecla and the History of Women in the Early Church* (New York: Oxford University Press, 2015), 23–31.

BIBLIOGRAPHY

Primary Sources

Anon. *Historia Augusta.* Translated by David Magie. Loeb Classical Library 139. Cambridge, Mass.: Harvard University Press, 1921.

Anon. "Joseph and Aseneth." Pages 177–247 in *The Old Testament Pseudepigrapha.* Edited by James H. Charlesworth. New York: Doubleday, 1985.

Appian. *Roman History.* Translated by Horace White. Loeb Classical Library. New York: Macmillan, 1913.

Apuleius. *Metamorphoses.* Translated by J. Arthur Hanson. Loeb Classical Library 44. Cambridge, Mass.: Harvard University Press, 1989.

Aulus Gellius. *Attic Nights.* Translated by John C. Rolfe. Loeb Classical Library 200. Cambridge, Mass.: Harvard University Press, 1927.

Cicero. *Pro Caelio.* Translated by R. Gardner. Loeb Classical Library 447. Cambridge, Mass.: Harvard University Press, 1958.

———. *Tusculan Disputations.* Translated by J. E. King. Loeb Classical Library 141. Cambridge, Mass.: Harvard University Press, 1945.

Galen. *On the Usefulness of the Parts of the Body.* Translated by Margaret Tallmadge May. Ithaca, N.Y.: Cornell University Press, 1961.

Juvenal. *Juvenal and Persius.* Translated by Susanna Morton Braund. Loeb Classical Library 91. Cambridge, Mass.: Harvard University Press, 2004.

Livy. *Histories.* Translated by B. O. Foster. Loeb Classical Library. Cambridge, Mass.: Harvard University Press, 1919.

———. *Histories.* Translated by Evan T. Sage. Loeb Classical Library. Cambridge, Mass.: Harvard University Press, 1935.

Martial. *Epigrams.* Translated by D. R. Shackelton Bailey. Cambridge, Mass.: Harvard University Press, 1993.

Ovid. *Ex Ponto.* Translated by Arthur Leslie Wheeler. Loeb Classical Library. New York: G. P. Putnam's Sons, 1924.

Philo. *On the Special Laws.* Translated by F. H. Colson. Loeb Classical Library. Cambridge, Mass.: Harvard University Press, 1968.

Plutarch. "Advice to the Bride and Groom." Pages 5–13 in *Plutarch's Advice to the Bride and Groom and A Consolation to His Wife: English Translations, Commentary, Interpretive Essays, and Bibliography.* Edited by Sarah B. Pomeroy. New York: Oxford University Press, 1999.

———. *Moralia.* Translated by Frank Cole Babbitt. Loeb Classical Library. New York: G. P. Putnam's Sons, 1927.

———. *Moralia.* Translated by Harold North Fowler. Loeb Classical Library 321. Cambridge, Mass.: Harvard University Press, 2005.

———. *Moralia.* Translated by W. C. Helmbold. Loeb Classical Library 337. Cambridge, Mass.: Harvard University Press, 2005.

Pseudo-Philo. "Biblical Antiquities." *The Old Testament Pseudepigrapha.* Edited by James H. Charlesworth. New York: Doubleday, 1985.

Suetonius. *The Twelve Caesars.* Translated by Robert Graves and J. B. Rives. London: Penguin, 2007.

Tacitus. *Agricola.* Translated by M. Hutton and R. M. Oglivie. Loeb Classical Library 35. Cambridge, Mass.: Harvard University Press, 1970.

———. *Dialogues on Oratory.* Translated by W. Peterson and M. Winterbottom. Loeb Classical Library 35. Cambridge, Mass.: Harvard University Press, 1970.

Valerius Maximus. *Memorable Doings and Sayings.* Translated by D. R. Shackelton Bailey. Loeb Classical Library 493. Cambridge, Mass.: Harvard University Press, 2000.

Xenophon of Ephesus. "An Ephesian Tale." *Collected Ancient Greek Novels*. Edited by B. P. Reardon. Berkeley: University of California Press, 1989.

Secondary Sources

Ackerman, David A. *1&2 Timothy, Titus*. Kansas City, Mo.: Beacon Hill Press, 2016.

Babcock, Charles L. "The Inscriptions." Pages 90–104 in *The Collection of Antiquities of the American Academy in Rome*. Edited by Larissa Bonfante and Helen Nagy. Ann Arbor: University of Michigan Press, 2015.

Bagnall, Roger S., and Raffaella Cribiore. *Women's Letters from Ancient Egypt, 300 BC–AD 800*. Ann Arbor: University of Michigan Press, 2006.

Bassler, Jouette. *1 Timothy, 2 Timothy, Titus*. Abingdon New Testament Commentaries. Nashville: Abingdon, 1996.

Bourdieu, Pierre. *Outline of a Theory of Practice*. Translated by Richard Nice. Cambridge: Cambridge University Press, 1977.

Bowman, Alan K. "Literacy in the Roman Empire: Mass and Mode." Pages 119–131 in *Literacy in the Roman World*. Edited by J. H. Humphrey. Ann Arbor: Journal of Roman Archaeology, 1991.

Bradley, Keith R. "Wet-nursing at Rome: A Study in Social Relations." Pages 201–229 in *The Family in Ancient Rome*. Edited by Beryl Rawson. Ithaca, N.Y.: Cornell University Press, 1986.

Brewer, David Instone. "Jewish Women Divorcing Their Husbands in Early Judaism: The Background to Papyrus Se'elim 13." *Harvard Theological Review* 92 (1999): 349–357.

Brooten, Bernadette J. *Women Leaders in the Ancient Synagogue: Inscriptional Evidence and Background Issues*. Brown Judaic Studies 36. Chico, Calif.: Scholars Press, 1982.

Buszard, Bradley. "The Speech of Greek and Roman Women in Plutarch's Lives." *Classical Philology* 105, no. 1 (2010): 83–115.

Castelli, Elizabeth. "Virginity and Its Meaning for Women's Sexuality in Early Christianity." *Journal of Feminist Studies in Religion* 2 (1986): 62–88.

Chesnutt, Randall D. "Revelatory Experiences Attributed to Biblical Women in Early Jewish Literature." Pages 107–125 in *"Women*

Like This": New Perspectives on Jewish Women in the Greco-Roman World. Edited by Amy-Jill Levine. Atlanta: Scholars Press, 1991.

Clark, Elizabeth A. *Women in the Early Church.* Message of the Fathers of the Church 13. Collegeville, Minn.: Liturgical Press, 1983.

Collins, Raymond F. *1 & 2 Timothy and Titus: A Commentary.* New Testament Library. Louisville: Westminster John Knox Press, 2002.

Cooley, Alison E. "Women Beyond Rome: Trend Setters or Dedicated Followers of Fashion?" Pages 23–46 in *Women and the Roman City in the Latin West.* Edited by Emily A. Hemelrijk and Greg Woolf. Leiden: Brill, 2013.

Cooper, Kate. "Closely Watched Households: Visibility, Exposure and Private Power in the Roman *Domus.*" *Past and Present* 197 (2007): 3–33.

Cotton, Hannah. "A Cancelled Marriage Contract from the Judean Desert." *Journal of Roman Studies* 84 (1994): 64–86.

Creanga, Ovidiu. *Men and Masculinity in the Hebrew Bible and Beyond.* The Bible in the Modern World 33. Sheffield: Sheffield Phoenix Press, 2010.

Cribiore, Raffaella. *Gymnastics of the Mind: Greek Education in Hellenistic and Roman Egypt.* Princeton: Princeton University Press, 2001.

Crook, Zeba. "Honor, Shame, and Social Status Revisited." *Journal of Biblical Literature* 128 (2009): 591–611.

Davies, Margaret. *The Pastoral Epistles.* New Testament Guides. Sheffield: Sheffield Academic Press, 1996.

de Certeau, Michel. *The Practice of Everyday Life.* Translated by Steven Rendall. Berkeley: University of California Press, 1984.

Dixon, Suzanne. "A Family Business: Women's Role in Patronage and Politics at Rome 80–44 B.C." *Classica et Mediaevalia* 34 (1983): 91–112.

———. *The Roman Mother.* Norman: University of Oklahoma Press, 1988.

———. "A Woman of Substance: Iunia Libertas of Ostia." *Helios* 19 (1992): 162–174.

Donahue, John F. "Iunia Rustica of Cartima: Female Munificence in the Roman West." *Latomus* 63 (2004): 873–891.

Evans Grubbs, Judith. *Women and the Law in the Roman Empire: A Sourcebook on Marriage, Divorce, and Widowhood.* London: Routledge, 2002.

Fantham, Elaine, Helene Peet Foley, Natalie Boymel Kampen, Sarah B. Pomeroy, and H. A. Shapiro. *Women in the Classical World: Image and Text.* New York: Oxford University Press, 1994.

Fertik, Harriet. "Privacy and Power: The *De Clementia* and the Domus Aurea." Pages 17–29 in *Public and Private in the Roman House and Society.* Edited by Kaius Tuori and Laura Nissin. Portsmouth, R.I.: Journal of Roman Archaeology, 2015.

Fiore, Benjamin. *The Pastoral Epistles: First Timothy, Second Timothy, Titus.* Sacra Pagina 12. Collegeville, Minn.: Liturgical Press, 2007.

Forbis, Elizabeth P. *Municipal Virtues in the Roman Empire: The Evidence of Italian Honorary Inscriptions.* Stuttgart: B. G. Teubner, 1996.

Gardner, Jane F. "Gender-Role Assumptions in Roman Law." *Echos du Monde Classique* 39 (1995): 377–400.

———. "Women in Business Life: Some Evidence from Puteoli." *Acta Instituti Romani Finlandiae* 22 (1998): 11–27.

George, Michele. "Repopulating the Roman House." Pages 299–319 in *The Roman Family in Italy: Status, Sentiment, Space.* Edited by Beryl Rawson and Paul Weaver. Oxford: Clarendon Press, 1997.

Graybill, Riannon. *Are We Not Men? Unstable Masculinity in the Hebrew Prophets.* New York: Oxford University Press, 2016.

Hallett, Judith P. *Fathers and Daughters in Roman Society: Women and the Elite Family.* Princeton: Princeton University Press, 1984.

———. "Perspectives on Roman Women." Pages 132–144 in *From Augustus to Nero: The First Dynasty of Imperial Rome.* Edited by Ronald Mellor. East Lansing: Michigan State University Press, 1990.

Halperin, David M. *One Hundred Years of Homosexuality and Other Essays on Greek Love.* New York: Routledge, 1990.

Hanson, Ann Ellis. "Ancient Illiteracy." Pages 159–198 in *Literacy in the Roman World.* Edited by J. H. Humphrey. Ann Arbor: Journal of Roman Archaeology, 1991.

Harland, Philip A. "Familial Dimension of Group Identity (II): 'Mothers' and 'Fathers' in Associations and Synagogues of the Greek World." *Journal for the Study of Judaism* 38 (2007): 57–79.

Helen, Tapio. *Organization of Roman Brick Production in the First and Second Centuries A.D.: An Interpretation of Roman Brick Stamps.* Annales Academiae Scientiarum Fennicae Dissertationes

Humanarum Litterarum 5. Helsinki: Academia Scientiarum Fennica, 1975.

Hemelrijk, Emily A. "Female Munificence in the Cities of the Latin West." Pages 65–84 in *Women and the Roman City in the Latin West*. Edited by Emily A. Hemelrijk and Greg Woolf. Leiden: Brill, 2013.

———. *Hidden Lives, Public Personae: Women and Civic Life in the Roman West*. New York: Oxford University Press, 2015.

Holleran, Claire. "Women and Retail in Roman Italy." Pages 313–330 in *Women and the Roman City in the Latin West*. Edited by Emily Hemelrijk and Greg Woolf. Leiden: Brill, 2013.

Holmes, Brooke. *Gender: Antiquity and Its Legacy*. New York: Oxford University Press, 2012.

Hopkins, Keith. "Contraception in the Roman Empire." *Comparative Studies in Society and History* 8 (1965): 124–151.

Horbury, William, and David Noy. *Jewish Inscriptions of Graeco-Roman Egypt*. Cambridge: Cambridge University Press, 1992.

Hylen, Susan E. *A Modest Apostle: Thecla and the History of Women in the Early Church*. New York: Oxford, 2015.

Ilan, Tal. "Women's Archives in the Judean Desert." Pages 755–760 in *The Dead Sea Scrolls Fifty Years after Their Discovery*. Edited by Lawrence H. Schiffman, Emanuel Tob, and James C. VanderKam. Jerusalem: Israel Exploration Society, 2000.

Johnson, Luke Timothy. *The First and Second Letters to Timothy: A New Translation with Introduction and Commentary*. Anchor Bible 35A. New York: Doubleday, 2001.

Jones, Arnold Hugh Martin. *The Greek City from Alexander to Justinian*. Oxford: Clarendon Press, 1940.

Jongman, Willem M. "The Early Roman Empire: Consumption." Pages 592–618 in *The Cambridge Economic History of the Greco-Roman World*. Edited by Walter Scheidel, Ian Morris, and Richard Saller. Cambridge: Cambridge University Press, 2007.

Joshel, Sandra R. "Nurturing the Master's Child: Slavery and the Roman Child-Nurse." *Signs* 12, no. 1 (1986): 3–22.

Kalmanofsky, Amy. *Gender-Play in the Hebrew Bible: The Ways the Bible Challenges Its Gender Norms*. London: Routledge, 2017.

Kampen, Natalie Boymel. *Image and Status: Roman Working Women in Ostia*. Berlin: Gebr. Mann Verlag, 1981.

Keady, Jessica M. *Vulnerability and Valour: A Gendered Analysis of Everyday Life in the Dead Sea Scrolls Communities.* Library of Second Temple Studies 91. London: Bloomsbury T&T Clark, 2017.

Kearsley, Rosalinde A. "Asiarchs, *Archiereis*, and the *Archiereiai* of Asia." *Greek, Roman and Byzantine Studies* 27 (1986): 183–192.

———. "Women and Public Life in Imperial Asia Minor: Hellenistic Tradition and Augustan Ideology." *Ancient West and East* 4 (2005): 91–121.

———. "Women in Public Life in the Roman East: Iunia Theodora, Claudia Metrodora and Phoebe, Benefactress of Paul." *Tyndale Bulletin* 50 (1999): 189–211.

King, Helen. *Hippocrates' Woman: Reading the Female Body in Ancient Greece.* London: Routledge, 1998.

———. *The One-Sex Body on Trial: The Classical and Early Modern Evidence.* Burlington, Vt.: Ashgate, 2013.

Kloppenborg, John S. "Edwin Hatch, Churches and *Collegia*." Pages 212–238 in *Origins and Method: Towards a New Understanding of Christianity and Judaism.* Edited by Bradley H. McLean. Journal for the Study of the New Testament Supplement Series 86. Sheffield: Sheffield Academic Press, 1993.

Kraemer, Ross Shepard. "Non-Literary Evidence for Jewish Women in Rome and Egypt." Pages 85–101 in *Rescuing Creusa: New Methodological Approaches to Women in Antiquity.* Edited by Marilyn Skinner. Lubbock: Texas Tech University Press, 1987.

———. *Unreliable Witnesses: Religion, Gender, and History in the Greco-Roman Mediterranean.* Oxford: Oxford University Press, 2011.

———. *Women's Religions in the Greco-Roman World: A Sourcebook.* Oxford: Oxford University Press, 2004.

Krause, Deborah. *1 Timothy.* London: T&T Clark, 2004.

Krause, Jens-Uwe. *Witwen und Waisen im Römischen Reich, 1: Verwitwung und Wiederverheiratung.* Stuttgart: Franz Steiner Verlag, 1994.

Langlands, Rebecca. *Sexual Morality in Ancient Rome.* Cambridge: Cambridge University Press, 2006.

Laqueur, Thomas. *Making Sex: Body and Gender from the Greeks to Freud.* Cambridge, Mass.: Harvard University Press, 1990.

Lefkowitz, Mary R., and Maureen B. Fant. *Women's Life in Greece and Rome: A Source Book in Translation*. 2nd ed. Baltimore: Johns Hopkins University Press, 1992.

Lightman, Majorie, and William Zeisel. "Univira: An Example of Continuity and Change in Roman Society." *Church History* 46 (1977): 19–32.

Lloyd, G. E. R. "The Hot and the Cold, the Dry and the Wet in Greek Philosophy." *Journal of Hellenic Studies* 84 (1964): 92–106.

MacMullen, Ramsay. "Woman in Public in the Roman Empire." *Historia: Zeitschrift für alte Geschichte* 29, no. 2 (1980): 208–218.

Madigan, Kevin, and Carolyn Osiek. *Ordained Women in the Early Church: A Documentary History*. Baltimore: Johns Hopkins University Press, 2005.

Magie, David. *Roman Rule in Asia Minor to the End of the the Third Century after Christ*. 2 vols. Princeton: Princeton University Press, 1950.

Malherbe, Abraham J. "How to Treat Old Women and Old Men: The Use of Philosophical Traditions and Scripture in 1 Timothy 5." Pages 263–290 in *Scripture and Traditions*. Edited by Patrick Gray and Gail R. O'Day. Leiden: Brill, 2008.

Marshall, Jill. *Women Praying and Prophesying: Gender and Inspired Speech in First Corinthians*. Atlanta: Emory University, Electronic Theses and Dissertations, 2015.

Martin, Dale B. *The Corinthian Body*. New Haven: Yale University Press, 1995.

———. "Slave Families and Slaves in Families." Pages 207–230 in *Early Christian Families in Context: An Interdisciplinary Dialogue*. Edited by David L. Balch and Carolyn Osiek. Grand Rapids, Mich.: William B. Eerdmans, 2003.

McDowell, Markus. *Prayers of Jewish Women: Studies of Patterns of Prayer in the Second Temple Period*. Wissenschaftliche Untersuchungen zum Neuen Testament 2. Reihe 211. Tübingen: Mohr Siebeck, 2006.

McGinn, Thomas A. J. *Prostitution, Sexuality, and the Law in Ancient Rome*. New York: Oxford University Press, 1998.

McLaren, Angus. *A History of Contraception: From Antiquity to the Present Day*. Oxford: Basil Blackwell, 1990.

Merkelbach, R., and S. Sahin. "Die publizierten Inschriften von Perge." *Epigraphica Anatolica* 11 (1988): 99–169.

Meyers, Eric M. "The Problems of Gendered Space in Syro-Palestinian Domestic Architecture: The Case of Roman-Period Galilee." Pages 44–69 in *Early Christian Families in Context: An Interdisciplinary Dialogue*. Edited by David L. Balch and Carolyn Osiek. Grand Rapids, Mich.: William B. Eerdmans, 2003.

Milnor, Kristina. *Gender, Domesticity, and the Age of Augustus: Inventing Private Life*. Oxford: Oxford University Press, 2005.

Moore, Stephen D., and Janice Capel Anderson. *New Testament Masculinities*. Semeia Studies 45. Altanta: SBL Press, 2003.

Mueller, Ilse. "Women in the Roman Funerary Inscriptions." *Zeitschrift für Papyrologie und Epigraphik* 175 (2010): 295–303.

Osiek, Carolyn. "Family Matters." Pages 201–220 in *Christian Origins*. Edited by Richard A. Horsley. Minneapolis: Fortress Press, 2005.

———. "The Family in Early Christianity: 'Family Values' Revisited." *Catholic Biblical Quarterly* 58 (1996): 1–25.

———. "The Patronage of Women in Early Christianity." Pages 173–192 in *A Feminist Companion to Patristic Literature*. Edited by Amy-Jill Levine. New York: T & T Clark, 2008.

Osiek, Carolyn, and Margaret Y. MacDonald. *A Woman's Place: House Churches in Earliest Christianity*. Minneapolis: Fortress Press, 2006.

Oudshoorn, Jacobine G. *The Relationship between Roman and Local Law in the Babatha and Salome Komaise Archives: General Analysis and Three Case Studies on Law of Succession, Guardianship and Marriage*. Studies on the Texts of the Desert of Judah 69. Leiden: Brill, 2007.

Pagels, Elaine. *The Gnostic Gospels*. New York: Random House, 1979.

Peskowitz, Miriam Beth. *"The Work of Her Hands": Gendering Everyday Life in Roman-Period Judaism in Palestine (70–250 C.E.), Using Textile Production as a Case*. Ann Arbor: UMI Dissertation Services, 1993.

Pudsey, April. "Death and the Family: Widows and Divorcées in Roman Egypt." Pages 157–180 in *Families in the Roman and Late Antique Roman World*. Edited by Mary Harlow and Lena Larsson Lonén. New York: Continuum, 2012.

Rawson, Beryl. *Children and Childhood in Roman Italy*. Oxford: Oxford University Press, 2003.

Richardson, Peter. "Early Synagogues as Collegia in the Disapora and Palestine." Pages 90–109 in *Voluntary Associations in the Greco-Roman World*. Edited by John S. Kloppenborg and Stephen G. Wilson. London: Routledge, 1996.

Roth, Ulrike. "Inscribed Meaning: The Vilica and the Villa Economy." *Papers of the British School at Rome* 72 (2004): 101–124.

Rowlandson, Jane, ed. *Women and Society in Greek and Roman Egypt: A Sourcebook*. Cambridge: Cambridge University Press, 1998.

Saarinen, Risto. *The Pastoral Epistles with Philemon & Jude*. Brazos Theological Commentary on the Bible. Grand Rapids, Mich.: Brazos Press, 2008.

Saller, Richard P. "*Familia, Domus*, and the Roman Conception of the Family." *Phoenix* 38 (1984): 336–355.

———. "Men's Age at Marriage and Its Consequences in the Roman Family." *Classical Philology* 82 (1987): 21–34.

———. "Pater Familias, Mater Familias, and the Gendered Semantics of the Roman Household." *Classical Philology* 94, no. 2 (1999): 182–197.

———. *Patriarchy, Property, and Death in the Roman Family*. Cambridge: Cambridge University Press, 1994.

———. "*Pietas*, Obligation and Authority in the Roman Family." Pages 393–410 in *Alte Geschichte und Wissenschaftsgeschicht e: Festchrift für Karl Christ zum 65. Geburtstag*. Edited by Peter Kneissl and Volker Losemann. Darmstade: Wissenschaftliche Buchgesellschaft, 1988.

Schremer, Adiel. "How Much Jewish Polygyny in Roman Palestine?" *Proceedings of the American Academy for Jewish Research* 63 (1997–2001): 181–223.

Schüssler Fiorenza, Elisabeth. *In Memory of Her: A Feminist Theological Reconstruction of Christian Origins*. New York: Crossroads, 1988.

Setälä, Päivi. "Women and Brick Production—Some New Aspects." Pages 181–199 in *Women, Wealth and Power in the Roman Empire*. Edited by Päivi Setälä, Ria Berg, Riikka Hälikkä, Minerva Keltanen, Janne Pölönen, and Ville Vuolanto. Rome: Acta Instituti Romani Finlandiae, 2002.

Severy, Beth. *Augustus and the Family at the Birth of the Roman Empire*. New York: Routledge, 2003.

Shelton, Jo-Ann. *As the Romans Did.* 2nd ed. New York: Oxford University Press, 1998.

Smith, Ted A. *The New Measures: A Theological History of Democratic Practice.* Cambridge: Cambridge University Press, 2007.

Swidler, Ann. *Talk of Love: How Culture Matters.* Chicago: University of Chicago Press, 2001.

Tanner, Kathryn. *Theories of Culture: A New Agenda for Theology.* Guides to Theological Inquiry. Minneapolis: Fortress Press, 1997.

Taylor, Charles. "To Follow a Rule..." Pages 45–60 in *Bourdieu: Critical Perspectives.* Edited by Craig Calhoun, Edward LiPuma, and Moishe Postone. Chicago: University of Chicago Press, 1993.

Treggiari, Susan. "Divorce Roman Style: How Easy and How Frequent Was It?" Pages 31–46 in *Marriage, Divorce, and Children in Ancient Rome.* Edited by Beryl Rawson. Oxford: Clarendon Press, 1991.

———. "Jobs for Women." *American Journal of Ancient History* 1 (1976): 76–104.

———. "Jobs in the Household of Livia." *Papers of the British School at Rome* 43 (1975): 48–77.

———. *Roman Marriage: Iusti Coniuges from the Time of Cicero to the Time of Ulpian.* Oxford: Clarendon Press, 1991.

Trümper, Monika. "Material and Social Environment of Greco-Roman Households in the East: The Case of Hellenistic Delos." Pages 19–43 in *Early Christian Families in Context: An Interdisciplinary Dialogue.* Edited by David L. Balch and Carolyn Osiek. Grand Rapids, Mich.: William B. Eerdmans, 2003.

van Bremen, Riet. "A Family from Sillyon." *Zeitschrift für Papyrologie und Epigraphik* 104 (1994): 43–56.

———. *The Limits of Participation: Women and Civic Life in the Greek East in the Hellenistic and Roman Periods.* Amsterdam: J. C. Gieben, 1996.

Vander Stichele, Caroline, and Todd Penner. *Contextualizing Gender in Early Christian Discourse: Thinking Beyond Thecla.* London: T&T Clark, 2009.

Wallace-Hadrill, Andrew. *Rome's Cultural Revolution.* Cambridge: Cambridge University Press, 2008.

———. "The Social Structure of the Roman House." *Papers of the British School at Rome* 56 (1988): 43–97.

Williams, Craig A. *Roman Homosexuality: Ideologies of Masculinity in Classical Antiquity.* New York: Oxford University Press, 1999.

Winter, Bruce W. *Roman Wives, Roman Widows: The Appearance of New Women in the Pauline Communities.* Grand Rapids, Mich.: William B. Eerdmans, 2003.

Wood, Susan E. *Imperial Women: A Study in Public Images, 40 B.C.–A.D. 68.* Leiden: Brill, 1999.

INDEX OF PRIMARY SOURCES

Literary Sources

Papyri

TOPICAL INDEX